CAN YOU REALLY HEAR FROM GOD NOWADAYS?

Can You Really Hear From God Nowadays?

Naylee Bartlett

Pinsan Books

DEDICATION

I want to dedicate this book to my only daughter.

Lisa, I want to share with you the work of God in my life and in your life too when you were little and while you are young. I want you to value God highly in everything. May God bless you darling, keep on believing God. He's the best inheritance I could share with you. GOD BLESS YOU!

CONTENTS

ACKNOWLEDGEMENTS

(To God alone the glory)

I want to express my gratitude to my mum who shared with me some of the experiences I wrote in this book and who taught me when I was little to be humble, for the Lord blesses a person with a humble spirit. (Maraming salamat po Inay.)

To David, my husband; thank you so much for helping me with my work, reading the manuscript after your day's work and helping me with some of the grammar.

I also want to thank all the people mentioned in this book: my sisters: Leonor, Nida and Oying; my brothers: Fred, Marcos and Nol; Sheryl, my home group leader; and Lyn and Lesley, church members who prayed for me and expressed their visions with me.

Most of all, I am in awe of you Lord; for the wonderful experiences and the special care and protection you gave me ever since I was little. I thank you Lord for the happy moments you shared with me, the very words you revealed to me and for everything I have; my husband, and my daughter. Lord, I praise you and worship you, You are everything to me and everything I have ever had is from you. I love you O Lord; You are my strength....

INTRODUCTION

Growing up as a Catholic had a great significance for me; knowing that there is God, somewhere in heaven, and believing that if you are good it could give you an advantage in that, probably, God would take note of what you did, and it might be credited to you as a good work or righteousness and would be your gate pass to heaven. That God is somewhere in heaven looking at who is good and who is bad, not really knowing the whole truth. It is every Christian's assurance to know that God is alive and willing to participate in their everyday life. But if you never hear God, how can you continue in your faith? You could receive healing through someone's faith when they pray, without actually hearing from God for yourself. Most of the time God will speak to you as recognition of His existence and give you assurance you are on the right path of faith.

If you kept on talking to someone, no matter how annoying you were they would answer you; but if you talk to God, He will not just answer you with compassion and love but he will bless you and impart something to you. Sometimes you will know about some event before it happens, see Psalm 25:14: *The Lord confides in those who fear Him; He makes his covenant known to them*. If you draw near to God He will draw near to you. Talk to Him for He can hear you. He will never leave you nor forsake you. For me it all started when I opened my heart to God, talked to Him and expected Him with sincerity of heart to talk to me.

1

ANGELUS

I was born in a fairly big family, the youngest of seven. My parents were both Catholics and very proud to be in that religion. Although my father was not practising, my mother on the other hand was devout. I remember when I was about five or six my mum would gather us four younger children to kneel and pray at six o'clock every evening. We could hear the church bells ringing from where we lived; that's the time my mum called it *Angelus*. We would pray *Hail Mary, I Believe* and *Our Father* while she counted the rosary beads in her hand, maybe an hour of kneeling and praying. When we finished, I would turn to my mum, get her right hand, kiss it and say, 'Bless me mother,' then I would turn to my father and do the same thing. Only I had to wait for my dad to put his glass of gin down (or a cup of coffee on a good day) before he could bless me. This was the Filipino way of expressing respect for one's elders, which I believe is a tradition handed down to us by the Spaniards. They colonised our country for over three hundred years, leaving us the heritage of the Roman Catholic religion. (Filipino people had their own customs and traditions before the Spaniards came to settle and colonised our country. Our precolonial religion was called Animism, which is based on Hinduism and Buddhism. It is still practised today by a handful of the indigenous tribes.)

Praying with my mum did not go on for long; my brothers and sister stopped praying with us during the Angelus time because this was the only time they could play after coming home from school. I was never able to concentrate on praying with Mum after they stopped; hearing them enjoying themselves made me feel left out and I could not really pay any attention to my mum when we were praying. Although my mum had managed to persuade me to join her for a while, that didn't last long. Sometimes half way through praying time I would excuse myself pretending to go to the toilet and wouldn't come back to pray with her. I'd come downstairs and join in playing with my brothers and sisters, but they wouldn't let me; they knew when I started praying I had to be there till the end of our praying session. I could not wait to go to school because I knew I would be allowed to play then. So when I started going to school, the Angelus time for me ended; I would rather play than pray.

Nevertheless, Mum continued praying on her own during Angelus time for as long as I could remember. Dad on the other hand just loved watching us playing. We would argue sometimes because our older brother or sister would cheat on us. But Dad would not side with anyone; he just watched and laughed at us. He would only say something if we two younger ones got physically hurt.

When we were all very young, every time we got into trouble with Mum and Dad our older brother and sister always got the blame for it. But when we were a bit older, Mum would smack and pinch me if I caused any trouble for them. Looking back at it now I just chuckle and think to myself, *serves me right*.

* * *

Every weekend my two brothers, sister and I used to go to my father's field and help him to plant cassava, maize, peanuts and so on. We had to plant them all in a straight line; if Dad saw they were not straight we had to redo them. It was quite hard work for us little children, but we loved to be out there playing. My job was to put seeds in the holes three at a time then cover them. We used to spend hours playing out there. My brother, who is four years older, made a pretend house for us all out of bamboo sticks and dried grass. It helped us to feel we had a house of our own, a shade when the sun was too hot.

We used to get some food at home when Mum and Dad were having a nap in the afternoon, or we would dig up some of the plants we planted when they were ready for harvest and cook them before Dad could catch us. We used to pull up the peanut plants, pick some that we thought were ready, or open a few corn cobs to see if they had ripened, cook them in a used pineapple tin, eat them and plant what we pulled up back in the ground—all before Dad could catch us! But sometimes Dad would find out and we would get a good telling-off because we ruined the plants, which was food for us all too.

Sometimes my other sister, six years my senior, would join us in this small house; she used to help us buy some cookies and sweets. She was my favourite sister. If she could not bring me things that I wanted she would bring me anything; even just a multi-coloured rubber band would make me very happy. We really enjoyed our time together on that small house we called our own; it was such a fun time during my childhood.

But when I was growing up I hated it because I had to help with the household chores. Being the youngest in the family I always had to do as I was told, even by my sister who is only two years older than I am.

She was ever so clever; I could not beat her ways of making excuses not to wash the dishes or tidy up the table after lunch. When I was a bit older I used to make the same excuses as she did, but my mum caught me fibbing, and I could not get away with it— 'my eyes always told the truth,' Mum said. We called her 'O A' (over-acting). She was good at it, pretending she had tummy-ache or toothache; even Mum was convinced. She could have been a child actor in the western world; she would truly cry, making out her tooth was so painful and gums swollen, and this was just before the dinner ended.

It did not go unnoticed with my older brother who knew when she was acting; it always happened just before all of us had finished our meal.

After living in England for such a long time I have since found out that even though she is in her nineties my mum still prays at six o'clock every night. We were visiting her in February 2010 when I saw her go to her room and pray, and my sister who looks after her told me, 'Yes, Mum still prays every night at six o'clock in the evening.' So the Angelus time for my mum carries on.

2

FASCINATION

My mum used to take me along to church now and again on Sundays. I would sit next to her and watch all those sombre-looking people walking on their knees, praying with veils on their heads and rosaries in their hands. Although I got bored I had to wait and sit quietly. Sometimes Mum would walk on her knees too, from the entrance of the church to the altar. I would have to wait twice as long, but I would think to myself, *my mum's poor knees; all that grit from peoples shoes, it must be painful.* I never saw a man walk on his knees—they didn't want to look soft. The sitting and waiting put me off going to church but there was no escape; whenever she wanted company, and my older sister couldn't come with her, I had to go along with Mum.

As I grew up I noticed my mum would always pray in the middle of the night. She knelt and prayed three or even four times in the night sometimes—I wondered if she ever got to sleep. I heard her mention my brothers' and sisters' names in her prayers most of the time but not mine. (I slept in my mum's bed when I was little.) All Mum's attitude towards praying left me fascinated. *Did she ever get anything from it?* I used to ask myself. Just waking up in the middle of the night to go to the toilet was bad enough let alone getting up to pray. *How could she do it night after night?* I asked myself many times, and then one day Mum told us about her dream.... In her dream she had been to heaven... and saw many different kinds of flowers there.... She wanted to pick some of these flowers but she was not allowed to do so. This place was very beautiful; she had never seen anything like that before, not in real life anyway, she said. It was so peaceful and calm that she did not want to leave the place until she was reminded of us.

Hearing Mum's story I became more fascinated with her, and desperately wanted to have the same dream as hers so I prayed, 'Lord I wish, I wish I could see heaven just like Mum.' I prayed over and over again for a few nights. And then one night I had a dream. In my dream I was alone, standing in an unfamiliar place.... All of a sudden a man appeared next to me. 'Who is this man?' I said to myself, 'And what is he doing here?' He had long hair and wore a long white robe.

He extended his hand and said to me, 'Come.'

'Hold on,' I thought, 'he is a stranger.... Where is he going to take me? My mum warned me not to go with strangers.'

Nevertheless I reached out to him. I was about to step forward when something caught my attention; a narrow road, gloomy and dusty with a little flickering street light. There were quite a lot of people coming and going. I pointed this to the man who was with me but he said, 'NO, *this* is the way!'

He was leading me along to this very tiny criss-cross like wire, not even a path. I could only see it when my foot touched it. I thought it might hurt my feet, but it didn't so I continued walking with him. It was dark and there was no proper path in this place. The criss-cross wire only appeared when my little feet were on it. I could see rubble, thorns and bushes all around my feet.

At the end of my walk, right in front of me was a huge mountain. I asked the man if I had to climb up but he had disappeared. I looked back to find any route, but there was nothing; no path, no other visible way I could go to. I was standing for a while trying to find out how I could go back but there was no other way; I was worried I couldn't go home, I just had to climb this enormous mountain.

I looked from side to side to see what was beyond this mountain but I could not see a thing. This mountain was very high and extremely wide. What could I do? 'I will be stuck here forever if I don't do anything,' I mumbled to myself. So I decided I had to climb this mountain; I wouldn't be able to leave this place if I just stood here. There was no escape now, I had to do it.

It was such a struggle to reach the top. When I did, I came to a graveyard with a garden. I heard a voice call out, 'Visitor!' But I didn't see anyone, and the voice seemed different, it didn't sound spoken!

Then I saw a few ladies tending the garden. I looked around and the first thing that dawned on me was the calmness and peacefulness of this place. It was beautiful and serene and sunny, although the sun was not shining. I thought to myself, *This must be heaven.*

I looked about in the garden to pick some flowers, but I heard a voice say, 'NO!' I turned to see who was talking to me, no-one was near and everyone's back was turned. I carried on reaching for a flower, but a voice forbade me a second time, 'NO!' I turned around again but the ladies were exactly in the same place the first time I saw them; they continued what they were doing as before. Fascinated with how beautiful the flowers looked, I carried on reaching for one; I was very persistent. For the third time I heard the voice say, 'NO!' Again I turned around to see who was speaking to me but they were still far away from me.

By then I realised they knew my thoughts! Their thoughts were voices to me.... 'Oh no,' I gasped! They knew what I was thinking and I became aware of it. By this time one of the ladies came over. She was just standing next to me; we didn't exchange words or speak yet we understood each other. It was like that her thoughts were speech to me and vice versa. I heard another voice call out, 'Visiting time is over,' but I said to a lady who was with me, 'Please don't let me go, I don't want to go anywhere, I like it here, this is my home.' She didn't say anything, she walked along and I followed her. The next thing I knew I was at a graveyard for little children.

The lady who was looking after this place pointed out a tiny grave to me and said, 'This is your brother's.'

I thought, *A baby... as far as I know I am the youngest, who is this baby? I am sure there is no baby after me.* I didn't realise she knew what I was thinking until she said, 'Your mum told you all about him.' I looked at the grave and I thought hard, 'Oh yes, I remember,' I replied, 'my half-brother from her first husband; he died of the sort of illness that was prevalent during World War II.' I paused and continued, 'Mum told us she was absolutely devastated when this baby died, she loved him so much that she would not be able to forget him. He was such a lovely boy.' I told her the story that my mum told me, with a sigh. Then she pointed at the lines of candles nearby.

'Do you see that,' pointing at the shortest candle, 'that is yours... it is not your time yet.'

'Why is my candle the shortest one of all?' I asked. And it was burning rapidly I thought; so I stared at it for a while to see what would happen. Eventually it burned more slowly, and in the end the candle appeared to be the same length as when I first saw it.

'These candles belong to newborn babies,' she replied.

I was about eight or nine at that time. Then I woke up.... 'Mum! I reached heaven too,' I squealed at her when I woke up. 'And the lady in the graveyard showed me the grave of my brother.' (He died when he was a baby.)

I told Mum the whole story of my dreams. 'Everything seemed so real. I remember the time when you told us about your baby that died during the war. I only saw the grave, I didn't see his face,' I confessed with sadness.

This made me believe in heaven when I was little. Even now I still believe that, for the real story of my little brother's was known there. I believed this was not just an ordinary dream and I promised myself I would be back someday to stay there forever, not as a visitor.

3

LIFE'S LITTLE MIRACLES

When I was little we had several dogs, but there was a particular one that I liked most. My mum called it 'Raham.' I could play with him for hours pulling his tail, dressing him up, stroking him and so on and he wouldn't hurt me, unlike the other dogs that always bit me and growled at me. This one was the friendliest one of all and I loved him. One event that happened to him I could not forget was when I lost him.

There was a typhoon and flooding and Raham went missing. I looked for him and so did my dad but we could not find him. After three days I overheard my dad say, 'It must be dead by now, the dog will not survive the flood.'

I cried and prayed on that night, 'Lord I wish, I wish (that was the way I used to pray) that dog would come back in three days, so you would have the time to look for it.' On the third day after my prayer (this was about seven days since it went missing) I woke up and heard a tiny voice say, 'Take a look downstairs.' So I went downstairs; I saw my sister busy sweeping the yard, and yes my dog was curled up in the corner. When he saw me he got up, looked me in the eye, came forward limping, and went back into the corner.

I was so happy he was back, 'Thank you Lord,' I mumbled to myself. Then I heard a tiny voice again say, 'That is his second life.'

Now I know and I believe if you have any worry about anything at all, whether you are a child or adult, it doesn't matter if your problem is big or small, the Lord can move into your situation, if the prayer is from your heart. The only thing that matters to God, I believe, is your heart's concern.

* * *

One day my brother found a broken gold wedding ring. He mended it to fit my little finger and gave it to me. I was quite proud to own a gold ring; not many children my age would own one, so I cherished this ring; after all it was from my eldest brother whom I loved. One of my brothers wanted to borrow it once, but I didn't let him and we fought over it. I tore his shirt accidentally and he cried, so my dad took the ring from me and hung it on the corner of the wall. But after a few days, I managed to get it and used it again as before. Nobody seemed to bother me after that.

Once I was with my sister on the beach. There were some people about and we were all picking tiny clams, so Mum could sell them in the market to get some pocket money for us. When the tide came in I was the only one left. The water was up to my shoulders as I was trying to dig the sand to get more clams. The next minute I knew my ring was missing. How could I find this ring with the vastness of the sea and the tide so high? 'Please help me again.' I cried and prayed again, 'I wish, I wish I would find this ring.' This time I promised God if I ever found it I would never lose it again. I started picking up anything in the sea. However the sea was not calm, so I spent about fifteen or twenty minutes looking for it but to no avail, nevertheless I prayed again. So I started searching for it a second time, put my hand in the sand and there it was. The minute I found it I got out of the sea as quickly as I could.

I glanced back at the sea, how vast... how wide... and deep. I was extremely grateful I had my ring back. I know some would think it a coincidence, but if you are in the open sea and the sea is rough and you lose a tiny object you would know what I am talking about.

When I was fourteen years old I gave the ring to my cousin's board mate in Manila, because it became too small for me. I was looking after my cousin's son at the time and I left the ring as a souvenir for I knew I would not come back to their place again.

* * *

One day a little bone popped up on my wrist and I do not know how it happened. I woke up to see this little bone raised up on my wrist. I prayed for it from time to time but it didn't go away. Then one ordinary day as usual I was in the bathroom praying and I kept on looking at it. Every time I looked at it, it became smaller. So I prayed over and over again for maybe seven or more times—it was like a testing time, *is it going to sink in or what?* But for as many times as I prayed, every time I looked at it, it became smaller and smaller till it completely sank in, no more raised bone—just normal. I felt like saying to myself, 'Go on, just carry on praying, expect to see a result and there it is. It might have appeared as a very little miracle but who can do a little or big miracle but God alone? To us Christians are prayers, to God belongs the miracle, so praise Him.

* * *

I remember my mum used to wake up three or even four times at night to pray, when I was little, which has probably rubbed off on me. Eleven years ago, being on my own I decided to do the same. For my mum it was praying, but for me it was praying and reading my Bible at night.

Because I did not have a curtain rail or any proper curtain in my bedroom windows, just the nets, I used to use a torch for reading to avoid letting the neighbours or any passers-by see the light from my bedroom windows in the middle of the night.

Sometimes I purposely woke up, but sometimes I just woke up without any apparent reason. Thinking about it now, maybe it was because it was too bright in my bedroom and I couldn't really go to sleep properly. Since I did not have anyone to consider being disturbed when waking up at night, I did not have any problem doing it.

If you are asking, 'Didn't you feel tired when you woke up in the morning?' Of course I did, but praying and reading at night gave me such an opportunity, that while other people were sleeping, I could have a one to one with the Lord.... Some of my friends thought I may be feeling lonely being on my own, but the truth is when it was daytime I had this constant conversation with the Holy Spirit, or with God. And I felt it was worth waking up at night to talk to God. It was (is) a sacrifice worth doing.

Although it may still be silent at about six-thirty or seven in the morning, it is not the same as the stillness of the night, or the calmness of the early hours of the morning, when the Lord truly meets with you....

I bought two AA batteries for my torch, but after about three or four days using it, the light from it got slightly dimmer as I was trying to carry on reading. I thought to myself, *Oh no, is that all? I need to replace the batteries already!* (At that time I was on income support.) But while I was still thinking about it and turning the torch off and on again, I could see it get brighter again. And I forgot to replace the batteries because it never went dim ever since.

Only after I got married in 1997 did I notice that

the batteries went flat. Not straight away, maybe a month after David and I were married. He brought so many rechargeable batteries when he moved in. So I asked him, 'How long would normal batteries last, if you use them for reading for about three or four times at night?'

'I don't know,' he replied, 'maybe three or four days.'

I said to him, 'I just realised, **I only ever put batteries in my torch once and that was over two years ago**.' Clasping my hand over my mouth, I said, 'The Lord has blessed me! Wow, the Lord has blessed me…I can't believe it.' I was so excited.

I only remember again now in 2005. I could only compare this experience with the stories of the two widows and the miracles they experienced of the oil that kept on flowing and the flour that didn't run out for several years, through Elisha and Elijah's prophetic words to them. (See 2 Kings 4:1−7 & 1 Kings 17:8−16.)

If David and I hadn't got married maybe my torch would still be running on the first set of batteries. I thank you Lord for such an amazing, first-hand miracle experience.

I know if I had been supplied with the world's wealth I could never experience God's generous blessing, and I could never see God's Hand in my life in this way. I praise the God of heaven and earth who is, I would say, my super generous Daddy….

I may be poor in the eyes of the world, but I am

very rich with God's blessings, hallelujah!

4

FORTUNE TELLER

Growing up in a big family, I had the advantage of having a brother or a sister to play with. But my parents found it very difficult to give us everything we needed. So I used to do little odd jobs to get pocket money. I would gather a specific kind of grass on land that used to be my dad's salt farm, and sell it to my neighbours for their pigs. But they would pay me with sweet bread or sweets. I was not happy with their payments because it didn't matter if I gathered twice as much as normal, I still got sweet bread for it, so I stopped doing it in the end. I would catch tiny prawns instead and sell them to a prawn farm; I always got a lot of money for doing this.

We lived near the river, which was a good opportunity for me to catch tiny prawns. My dad told us the best time to get a good catch. This river was connected to the sea, so it was tidal. One day I was so eager to go and catch tiny prawns and the tide was just coming in. 'Perfect time to catch them,' I murmured. I was very excited knowing I would catch a lot of them. I could buy a new pair of shoes or maybe a tiny purse; I always liked the ones that looked like a miniature bag. First I had to sell them to the prawn farm for a few pesos once I had caught them. I continued daydreaming on the way to the river.

As I was getting closer I felt very strange. I felt a bit nervous! My enthusiasm was fading; I stopped and sensed for a while how my feelings had changed. Just ahead of me was a tiny footpath; standing on both sides were tall trees hiding me from the gaze of the people in the street and from home. Then I felt that my feet were getting heavy—I could hardly lift them. I was frightened to pass through the footpath. I pulled myself together and said to myself, 'I've been here many times, nothing has harmed me …. Once I pass through here I will be alright,' or would I be? I was interrupted by my thoughts; I tried to step forward but even my body felt ever so heavy…and my strength seemed as if it had been sapped away. I sensed within me I was in great danger. Then I heard a voice right inside me say, 'If you pass this way you will die, and it's your dad!' Immediately after I heard it, I felt goose bumps…. I gaped at the footpath; *why would he kill me…?* I tried to find an answer but nothing I could think of. I don't know if I had to believe the voice I heard or not, but even the hair on the back of my neck stood up. I was fearful with mixed emotions. So I decided to go to my dad's small, enclosed prawn farm instead, because I was too scared to go any further. I caught a few tiny prawns, and then I went home.

Later on that day, my dad came home carrying wood—fuel for my mum's cooking. The rest of the wood he used to sell to anyone who wanted it, like bakers and ordinary people. Then I saw him sharpening his bolo. He asked me why I didn't go in the river to catch the tiny prawns. 'I don't know,' I replied, 'I felt my feet were so heavy and I could not move, so I went home.'

'Your guardian angel is watching over you,' he said in reply to me. I didn't know about guardian angels at that time. I didn't know what he meant so I did not say anything and I forgot the whole event. For a few days I was frightened to pass on that footpath.

* * *

Life continued, I grew up, and in 1982 I graduated from high school. During that time I became a born-again Christian. I pursued further studies and went to college but I didn't finish my degree. Even in these early days of becoming a born-again Christian I could hear God respond to me.

I had a pain in the back of my neck once. During a prayer meeting the pastor called out for anyone who wanted to be healed or just to receive a touch from God. I put my hand up, and this was the first time I really felt the touch of God. I knew it was He…. The pastor told us to place our left hand where the pain was and lift our right hand to receive healing from God.

As we were praying I felt someone was beside me

passing by, and I felt a very, very gentle press on my left thumb; then the pain was completely gone. So I opened my eyes to thank the person who prayed for me. But everyone's eyes were closed and no one was laying hands on anybody. Everyone was standing still and responding to the leading of the pastor's praying. I am sure it was the Lord himself who touched me; I had never felt a touch so gentle, it was inexpressible; and I never know if I will ever feel a direct physical touch from God again, but I am content with my experience. I never even gave a testimony for my healing that I received from God. I was a new member of this church and I never had an opportunity to express it, though I did thank God in my own way for healing me.

It was also at this time when I kept on praying, 'Lord, I want to see you.' I kept on and on for quite some time day and night; I just had this urge of wanting to see Him. I thought, *What would He look like? Would He be the same as the one I always saw in the Catholic Church buildings, would I recognise Him?* I was still a new Christian and it seemed so impossible to tell anyone about what I was asking. I couldn't suggest that request at a prayer meeting. But between me and God personally I asked Him when I prayed, 'I want to see You Lord Jesus, Father God' and I would cry in my request to show me what He looked like; something like a craving of my heart to see Him....It is not that I did not believe He existed, it was just I badly wanted to see Jesus.

One afternoon my sister was planning to see me. I cannot remember what for, but I was praying for hours on that day and maybe had been for weeks and weeks to see God's face, then I stopped praying. I was staying at my eldest sister's house; she had just married an Englishman a few months back and my dad had asked me to stay with them just to help, even if it was just doing some shopping for them because my brother-in-law was finding it difficult to get used to the tropical climate.

I went out from the sitting room and I saw two faces of Jesus. When I saw them, I said to myself, 'What is this?' The Lord said, 'You wanted to see me, but don't tell anyone....' One of my sisters just arrived seeing me full of tears in my eyes, asking me what was wrong; I said nothing, 'But why are you crying?' she demanded. 'Are you mad? You wouldn't be crying without any reason at all.'

So I explained to her I had been praying for weeks now to see the Lord Jesus and I just saw Him in two forms, but He said not to tell anyone.... 'And here I am telling you all about Him....' The first one was dressed up in white, looking really gaunt and really thin, full of sufferings, bags under His eyes and you would never see any attraction in Him. But one thing I noticed He had the most compassionate eyes I have ever seen in my life. And in the second form he looked normal and healthy with brown hair down to His shoulders and wearing a sort of reddish wine-coloured robe. I saw just the half body in my sister's kitchen/ dining room.

At that time my sister, whom I was staying with, was busy burning the rubbish outside in the garden. There was no rubbish collector in my country at that time; only in recent years did the government provide a truck which picked up the rubbish once a week, at least in my hometown....

My sister had just finished burning all this rubbish and was about to go into the house, when I saw the second vision of the Lord. It was as though He was coming indoors, just ahead of my sister—so I could have opened the door for Him I felt. But I stopped myself doing it because my sister might have thought it strange as I had never done it for her before, because obviously she couldn't see the Lord just a few steps ahead of her....

After that I felt I didn't let God in my sister's house—I just didn't want my sisters to think that because I had become a born-again Christian I had flipped.... I was aware of what they would think of me and what would they say; I was saving myself from what they might insinuate. I look back now and think to myself, it's typical of me, not letting the Lord into my house because I wasn't sure of what my sisters would think of me; fear of what others would say, especially during those years....

* * *

On the 6th of September 1986 I went to reside in

England. After living here for over nine years, I went to visit my sister in Greece. I hadn't seen her for all those years and I missed her terribly because we had so much in common. We had the same sense of humour and we were very close. Exchanging letters and speaking over the telephone was not the same.

I arrived at three o'clock in the morning Greek time and we were both very tired; neither of us had slept that night. I suggested that my sister should take a nap, because she had work the following day and I wanted to get a rest myself, but my sister wouldn't let me. She said, 'I haven't seen you for over nine years, and I've got work later on.' She insisted we should talk so we chatted until she left for work. At last I could go to sleep. I sighed and off I went.

She didn't arrive till evening on that day, sleepless and tired but we started talking again about everything and anything: our childhood, brothers and sisters, and old jokes that still made us laugh after all those years.

This was three days after Christmas. I was really looking forward to spending the New Year with her. My sister had a few days off work and on New Year's day 1996 she gave me a song; it goes like this:

Let the Lord have His way, in your life everyday
There's no peace, there's no joy
Until the Lord have His way.

Put your life in His hands
Rest secure in His plans
Let the Lord, let the Lord have his way.

And then we talked about Mum and Dad. And I remembered the time when my dad wanted to kill me (I never told anyone about this situation before, to be honest I completely forgot). I do not know what made me remember it, but I did. So I told my sister the whole story, but she didn't seem surprised at all. I asked her if she knew why he wanted to kill me.

He had always told us that I was his favourite daughter when we were very young. When I was visiting my eldest sister two years earlier she had said the same thing, I was Dad's favourite. For a complete reversal of his action towards his claim I was stunned.

My sister told me that Dad had been to two different fortune tellers. When he visited the first one, this fortune teller told him that one of his youngest children was going to kill him. My dad believed in superstition, palm reading, tarot cards, and so on. Most Roman Catholics believed in these superstitions. He was so bothered about this finding that he went on to another fortune teller.

The second fortune teller said exactly the same thing, one of his youngest children was going to kill him. This, I believe, he took to heart. This scenario stayed on my mind for some time.

I am glad I did not have any grudge against my

dad; I felt no hatred or anger. I was somehow relieved that I knew now why he threatened to kill me. He had passed away by then. I also remember my brother telling me dad wanted to kill him when we were little but I did not believe him because I had forgotten my own experience.

My dad had always been a caring person, especially to us, his children, and loved us all equally. I am wondering now how he must have felt then? I knew for sure by this time my brother had forgotten the whole situation. Although I heard about the fortune tellers once or twice when I was little, I had been reminded again after my sister repeated the story to me. I vaguely remembered the conversation between Mum and Dad about the 'fortune teller's predictions.' I was very young when this event happened.

The reality was far from it; my dad died seven years ago of a severe asthma attack. Obviously the fortune teller's prediction was just one bad guess that nearly cost me my life; I really thank the Lord for saving me.

I do believe that God predestines our position here on earth—that is God's plan for our lives, but it depends on whether we are going to obey Him or not. God has a say in our lives here on earth. Our willingness and obedience are His joy.

5

CAN YOU REALLY HEAR FROM GOD NOWADAYS?

Before I came to England I was a child minder to a little girl who was born in the Philippines to Canadian parents, missionaries over there. I was a backslider at that time, as we Christians call it. But I would still fast and pray during that time. I didn't really turn my back on God completely, for I had known his goodness in my life ever since I was little. I always found a way of thanking Him in my own way as I was so grateful.

I arrived in the United Kingdom on Saturday, the 6th of September 1986. In the same street where I lived was a small Assemblies of God Pentecostal church, and by the summer of 1991 I had joined this local church here in England.

Going back to church again felt like another chapter of my life had been renewed. In this particular church the presence of God was tangible. On one occasion I asked someone to pray for me about fasting. I had promised God I would fast for two weeks and I could feel God was asking me to fulfil my promise. I had fasted many times before and tried many times to do it for up to two weeks but I just couldn't. It was a very difficult thing to do.

For a few months I felt the Lord was asking me, 'Where is your promise, when are you going to fulfil it?' This was a few years after I joined this church. I told a lady in the church about my promise to God, and how much I had tried to do it several times and how I failed to fulfil it. I simply told her I couldn't do it. But she insisted I had to do it. I thought she would be soft on me and would let me off, but I knew deep down it was so wrong of me to presume if it was all right with her, it would be all right with God.

What I vow to God is between God and me; in my own human reasoning, He is a God of love and He would let me off; in my heart I wanted an easy way out. I know one of the hardest things someone can do is to fast; it's worse than a famine, at least in a famine there is only a shortage of food, but in fasting there is food that is available for you but you cannot have it. You might have money to buy it, but you cannot eat it. If your actions don't condemn you, then I believe it would be all right, but I felt condemned and it was reflected in my heart attitude.

But God is a God of standards and I know He wouldn't ask me if He knew I could not do it. He is always faithful and generous and loving and kind and forgiving; He understands me fully and He knows all my weaknesses, furthermore my life is in His hands. I knew for sure I wouldn't die fasting. And He says: *He will never leave you nor forsake you* (Deuteronomy 31:6). *So where is my faith and trust in God?* I thought to myself.

This lady I asked responded with, 'Whatever you vow to God you must do it.'

So on that very day I started the fast for two weeks but I ended up doing it for twenty days, because I felt if this was borrowed money it would incur interest, and this was a vow to God that had lasted for over thirteen years before I even started doing it. My intention was for three weeks but on the twentieth day I could feel the Lord was telling me 'It's alright, you can stop now.' Even the Lord let me off a day.

I learned my lesson after this, not to make a promise to God if I could not fulfil it. And to be very careful of what I promise Him. So I declared to myself, 'I will never fast again.'

When I'm fasting I feel that I am humbling myself in the sight of God, and God alone. That is why, when it's possible, I avoid telling anyone.

After fasting, something had changed in me somehow; I had the desire to draw near to God. And I had peacefulness and happiness deep inside that I could not explain. I had hunger for His word, for praying, and for real communication with Him; just talking to Him as though talking to a friend. You might think it's sad but it is true. I felt He was drawing me close to Him. Sometimes when I read His word the pages of the Bible would turn pink. I'd sing praises to God when I woke up in the morning because I had a song in my heart. This carried on until 1996 when I could really hear God talking to me and I knew it was God.

On the 14th of May 1996 I went to my home group. (This is a group of Christian believers who would pray for each other's needs and socialise at the same time. The needs could be physical, spiritual, emotional, or even financial.) I asked the home group leader to pray for me as I was a bit down at the time, so she did; but the next thing she said amazed me....

'I have seen lots and lots of boxes for you, and the Lord will give you the desires of your heart.'

She felt the Lord wanted me to hear these words. I had so many wishes; I didn't actually know at that time what my heart's desire was. I didn't know what to say, because I never thought I would get a word from the Lord. I said to myself, 'What are the boxes for?'

When I went home I prayed and read my Bible and I asked the Lord to give me a word that I could stand on. I was expecting Him to answer me and after a few minutes right inside my heart this was what I heard: 'Wait patiently.'

I said, 'Lord, where would I see that in your Word?'

And He replied, 'Psalm 40:1.' So I turned my Bible to that verse and this was what it said: *I waited patiently for the Lord; He turned to me and heard my cry.*

I was very excited knowing I had heard the right words; I was elated for hearing it directly from God. So I decided to fast to thank Him for the word He gave me.

You see how easily I broke my promise not to fast again. This was also the year I fasted so often and felt God was softening my heart.

This year, 1996, was the most memorable for me, for this was the year I felt I had sat on God's lap.... One of the ladies in our home group commented once that I possessed a red phone book (direct line) from God. For whenever I prayed the answer was there. Sometimes I didn't even pray for it, it was just in my heart and the answer was there. This happened quite a lot. Every moment of the day I would talk to Him. For example, one day I was waiting for the bus and I whispered, 'Lord, I hope the bus will come on time.' And then I heard a voice reply, 'Five minutes.' I checked on my watch and exactly five minutes later the bus had arrived.

This voice was not audible so I could have ignored it. It wasn't from my mind either, but right deep inside my heart, then it went to my mind. I could sense it from my spirit. I knew it was from the Lord.

When I was meditating on God's goodness and communicating with Him silently, especially when I was in public places, the Lord would respond in His normal way. When I heard a word from God I would always check it; if it is in line with His Word then it's more likely to be from the Lord. Maybe there are words you wouldn't find in the Bible, like *five minutes*, but I know the Lord is spontaneous. The amazing thing the Lord can do is to speak at the precise time.

Most of the time I could sense something was going to happen before it actually did. It was so amazing. Occasionally I knew precisely what was going to happen although I only half believed it until it actually happened.

I felt so favoured in that year. I believe if one's heart is yearning to be close to God it doesn't matter who you are, it doesn't matter what your race is, your religious background or even your position in the community; if you call to the living God, the God who created the heaven and earth and everything in it, if you call to Him with all your heart, He will answer you.

For He said in Jeremiah 33:3: *Call to me and I will answer you and show you great and mighty things you never knew.*

On the 9th of June 1996 I asked the Lord for the second time to give me another word. The Lord said, 'Do not fret.'

'Lord where would I see that?' I asked.

'Psalm 37:1,' I heard Him say.

That scripture says, *Do not fret because of evil men or be envious of those who do wrong.*

I asked a friend to pray for me a few days after. While she was praying she saw a vision. She saw a man just passing by my path who shouldn't have been there.

And the other word was the story of the lady who

was subject to bleeding for twelve years; she said to herself, 'If I could only touch the hem of Jesus' garment I would be healed.'

These words fitted my circumstances at that time. I thank God for leading me for He knew my heart.

On the 11th of August of that year I was in Church feeling cold, although it was the height of summer, because I was fasting again. My home group leader told me she was praying for me the night before, and she saw in a vision lots and lots of boxes again, all nicely wrapped and decorated with ribbons and things and they were for me. She felt the Lord was telling me to receive a gift and that He had not finished dealing with me and something big was coming my way.

I went home puzzled not knowing what the boxes meant. And what did she mean by 'the Lord had not finished dealing with me?' *Had I done something wrong?* I asked myself. Yet I felt the Lord was leading me. I sensed in my spirit something I could not explain; I felt someone, somewhere in that church loved me....I knew the Lord does without a shadow of a doubt, but I also had a feeling of being in-love, but with no one in particular—it seemed total madness....

There was a certain person whose sister said he was interested in me but we hadn't even gone out together; we were not even friends as such. I was also trying to catch him out to see if his sister was telling the truth. He only said *hello* and smiled at me once. I never caught him looking at me so I was pretty certain his sister was joking. Nevertheless it didn't really matter because I didn't even fancy him.

We used to go bowling together with a friend and his sister but that was as far as it went, yet this feeling was so strange it seemed like madness. I did feel like this the first time I became a born-again Christian. But this was a few years since I came back to the Christian faith. Before I backslid those feelings had lasted for months, but this was two years since and still going strong.

This feeling of being loved, and in-love, with no one in particular was reclining heavily on me (it seemed stupid, but that's what I felt). I could not deny the reality that I was happy and contented on my own, because I felt loved by God....

Then one night as I was praying, I said to the Lord, 'Please Lord, captivate my heart that I wouldn't fall in love with anyone but you.' But I could see in a vision my left hand with a wedding ring.... I opened and closed my eyes four or five times while I was praying, and every time my eyes were closed I saw a wedding ring. 'But my prayer; O Lord, does this mean I am getting married? Or am I married to you?' (See Isaiah 54:5.) But the Lord didn't give me an answer on that day. At this stage of my life I was extremely frightened of any relationship, owing to a bad experience I had in the past.

On the 9th of October 1996 I was in bed asking the

Lord again to give me any word I could stand on. Almost immediately I heard the Lord say, 'Psalm 75:1.' So I opened my Bible and this was what it said: *We give thanks to you, O God, we give thanks for your name is near, men tell of your wonderful deeds.*

Once more I was puzzled; did I hear the right word? I kept on repeating the word *we...we*. I said to myself, 'It's hardly for me.' Then I asked the Lord, 'Why is it *we*, Lord?'

The Lord replied, 'DAVID'....I said, 'David...?' 'DAVID' He replied for the second time.... 'PRAY FOR HIM,' said the Lord. It was very, very clear. I didn't know what to pray. Looking at my Bible I said, 'If this is from you Lord, I am praying, 'I'm lifting up my right hand to you together with David's spiritual right hand.' And I recited the word the Lord gave me in Psalm 75:1. I ended with, 'I pray that you would bless him and protect him, let your will be done in his life, in Jesus' name Amen.' I am just thinking now; if I hadn't asked the Lord, 'Why it is *we*?' would the Lord have told me David's name? I suppose sometimes we definitely have to ask....

David was the person who operates the sound system in our church; he was the one I used to go bowling with, together with his sister and a friend. I was quite surprised that he didn't show any interest at all—although his sister had mentioned once he was interested in me. And everyone knew he was a shy type of person and was always busy every

Sunday, but I thought to myself, *There are other days of the week. If he really were that interested he would have said so.*

Six days after this I went to my home group. I never told anyone what I heard from God; well I thought this was personal. It was between God and me; I was also thinking of what others might say. They might not believe me; I had to keep it to myself for a little while. But I did mention to my home group leader in passing that he was interested in me.

I was a bit weepy on that day and three of the ladies prayed for me. Sheryl, my home group leader was the first one to pray and she said, 'Do you remember the boxes? The Lord wants you to open them. You felt that it was not for you but the Lord says, "Open it."' In natural circumstances this was completely ludicrous, because nothing was actually in front of me. How could I open invisible boxes? But we were dealing with a spiritual walk of faith. I knew that faith was the evidence of things we hope for and not of the natural things we could grasp hold of.

We all felt the presence of the Holy Spirit was tangible in the room on that day. The second lady Lynn, after she prayed said, 'I saw a vision of you, your head was bowed down, you were not sure of what was going on around you, then you looked up and you saw a brilliant light. It's from the Holy Spirit....' And the third lady, Lesley, after she prayed she said, 'You don't have to work hard to receive from God. The Lord is not cruel; he wouldn't take it away from you. It was given to you, therefore it's yours.'

One of the ladies gave a testimony that the Lord had healed her of the terrible pain she was suffering the night before; she couldn't go to sleep because of an illness that attacked her nerves. But after her husband prayed for her, she slept through the night and felt absolutely fine that morning and managed to come to our meeting. After hearing her testimony, I heard a whisper of the Holy Spirit, 'David will do the same, pray for you when you are not well.'

I was confused and frightened, and excited at the same time. Though I could not share my excitement with anyone, I could sense the Lord was with me. I knew the Lord told me David's name, not only on the ninth of October, but also right in that room. I didn't know what to think or to do. All I knew was what the ladies were telling me was connected to what I personally felt. I didn't dare tell anyone about David....

I went home confused. A few minutes after I arrived home the phone rang; it was my home group leader, again. She said she prayed for me after I left, and she felt that the Lord was telling me that I didn't want to open the present because I was frightened that I might give it back to Him (God).

'You have not been overlooked' were the next words she said. I paused and said to myself, 'Here is a lady repeating what I told God, my inner feelings, seconds before my phone rang.'

'I might give it to back to You' were the exact words that came out of my mouth....

That was incredible.... The Lord answered as well what I was thinking, because David didn't have a job then. That was what I thought when I heard the second word, 'You have not been overlooked.' Because I thought, *Why would the Lord give me an unemployed person knowing I was in the same position?*

I never understood David's sister when she told me he was interested in me, eight months ago. I didn't know if his feelings had changed by then. I only caught him once glancing at me, and he talked to me once when we were at a church picnic. So I didn't think anything more about him.

Then I fasted again to thank God for the words he gave me, and the confirmed word He told me through the ladies in my home group. For me, fasting was the way of humbling myself before God and saying thank you to Him. After all I do not have wealth to give and everything that surrounds us is from Him. The very breath in my nostrils was from Him; every single penny I ever had or spent is of the Lord's. All I could offer God was my heart, the very thing in me that the Lord could look into. 'May the meditation of my heart be acceptable to you, O Lord,' I usually prayed.

On the 6th of November 1996 I was fasting again and praying as usual, because I was frightened of how David's family and people from the church would react, knowing I am a foreigner. His mother and his sister knew me pretty well—but not his father. Yet the Lord gave me an assurance when He gave me His word during my fasting. In Isaiah 54:4 it says: *Do not be afraid; you will not suffer shame. Do not fear disgrace; you will not be humiliated.*

I didn't know much about his dad, as I'd never met him then. All I knew about him was that he went to the Brethren Church.

One day I was praying and I saw a man in a vision; he was lying on grassy ground wearing a green t-shirt. He had a slight Mediterranean appearance. I said to God, 'Lord who is he? What does he want? Can I pray for him?' He was very still. I asked the Lord, 'Is he dead?' He moved his head. The Lord replied, 'He's David's dad.' I didn't know what it meant and why the Lord would show him to me.

On Sunday the 10th of November 1996, we were in church and I told my home group leader that the Lord had given me a name of a person and he was a church member. I did not tell her who he was and I asked her not to tell a single living soul about it. At the following home group meeting she asked me to stay for lunch and to have a chat about this person; she guessed who it was before I told her.

Two weeks prior to this meeting they were teasing me about the audio tape that David gave me; we normally pay, but he refused to accept my money.

I had asked him for a copy of the words of prophecy and a song. They found out how easily I got it and for free, so they thought he favoured me. I just thought anyone who would ask for a copy of a tape would get it. I consoled myself with the thought that we went out bowling together so we were sort of friends.

Three weeks before this home group meeting, the church worship leader felt the Lord had a song for her to sing, but she could only sing it after a word of prophecy had been given. So she asked the congregation to come forward with a word of encouragement or prophecy to share with us. 'It is not a spooky time either.' She continued, 'If we wouldn't expect it, how could we flow as part of church life?' And this was the word of prophecy:

'I'M ENOUGH, I'M ENOUGH, I'M EL SHADDAI, AND I'M ENOUGH.' And the song goes like this:

In every situation I can be there, in every trial that you face.
In everything that comes against you, comes against me and you.
And I will be enough; I will be enough for you.

Give up your worry, give up your fretting.
Some of you are waiting for me to let you down.
Give up trying to find your help in other situations,

Look up and I'll come down to you.
I am enough for everything that comes against
you, I am enough.
For everything that threatens to overtake you
place me in the highest place and then go look
there first of all.
I'll be found of you and I will be enough.

Even before anyone could stand and give a word of prophecy she was already strumming the tune of the song, it was as incredible as that. I didn't realise the song was actually from the Lord. The worship team didn't know the lyrics of the song; I only found out when I spoke to my home group leader. Before she told us I thought the worship leader knew exactly what to sing when someone delivered a word of prophecy. After all she is a worship leader and she was friendly to the person who delivered the word. How wrong I was to presume because they were friends she knew what to sing.

A few more weeks had passed when my home group leader said, 'David ought to know.' She asked me if I would tell his sister. When I said no, she asked me if she could tell him. I told her I didn't believe that the Lord was dealing with me but not with him. I thought it wouldn't be fair if I told his sister; she might think I was making it up because of what she told me a few months back. Nevertheless I told his sister that the Lord gave me a name, but I didn't tell her who he was, because it wouldn't seem fair. I thought David would make a decision by force without really knowing if the Lord was telling him the same thing.

I didn't want to open up myself to any disgrace or humiliation. Although I heard the Lord clearly I didn't want to assume he had heard the same as I had.

On the 26th of November I was praying again; Sheryl felt I was asking the Lord what I had to do next. 'Be patient, wait and see,' was the word she told me. She thought that was the word the Lord wanted to tell me. It was true I was wondering what to do then. I asked her as well if she mentioned my situation to anyone. She said, 'Yes, I did. To the pastors.' And they told her they felt peace over it, which was good news for me. I wasn't so sure of everyone's reaction if it came out in the open.

I know some members of the church might think it was all fabricated and it was nothing to do with God. They would probably think we were just lonely people wanting to be together. Even my home group leader pretended to tease me by saying, 'Are you sure you heard David?' I simply told her, 'I know what I heard.' She even jokingly asked me if I didn't want to change my plan. 'Disobedience is wilful enmity against God,' I replied.

I don't want to be God's enemy, I'd rather be His friend. Now the Lord was showing me His will in my life, who was I to refuse? After all, I was the one who kept on asking God about His plan in my life. I wouldn't want to turn my back on Him. Just for a change now it's God's choice and not mine. I had made my choice before, and it was a complete disappointment.

I woke up in the middle of the night on the 2nd of December 1996. I could hear this word the Lord told me, 'Pray that you and David will not miss out on the blessing.' I sat up on my bed and said, 'If this is from you Lord I am praying that David and I will not miss out on the blessing you have for us, in Jesus' name, Amen.' I felt the blessing was not individual; I couldn't claim it without him and he couldn't claim it without me.

'Lord, just tell me what to say and I am going to tell him,' I muttered. 'I don't know if I have to tell him what you have told me. I just don't know how I would let him know.' But the Lord didn't say anything so I kept dead quiet about it.

On the 17th of December 1996 it was my 37th birthday. All day I had an absolutely strange feeling that I had never felt before or after. I felt I would receive something from David; maybe a card, a phone call, or something. It was truly bizarre; the reality was I didn't even know if he knew my birthday was on that day....It was very strange... he was not my boyfriend, we were not even friends as such; I didn't have any particular reason to expect anything from him. But why was I expecting something from him intensely, and profusely ignoring the reality of the situation? I said to myself, 'Wake up, why would he do that?' But this was what

I felt and I could not help it. It was so immense; my expectation was for real, and I said to myself, 'This is lunacy!'

Sometime on that afternoon I opened the door and outside I saw a white box and a card with my name on it; I was so excited believing it was from David. I went out quickly and took it, then I recognised my friend's handwriting; she had given me three delicious little cakes. But instead of being grateful, I felt a bit disappointed.

As the evening was drawing to a close, I became a bit disheartened and dissatisfied. So I went to my bedroom and prayed, read the word and talked to God. I asked the Lord why I felt the way I did. Why was it on my birthday and… why, why, why had I to expect anything from him? But despite the circumstances I had complete peace of mind and heart that something was going to happen. I never felt like that ever again, it was just on that day. After I finished talking to God my feelings had changed, I wasn't expecting anything anymore; somehow I was contented again and relaxed.

At about half past six at night, I was listening to gospel music when the telephone rang. I picked up the receiver and said hello; it was a male voice on the line… I didn't know who it was. For a split second I forgot my anxiety of the whole day. 'It's David; happy birthday!' he said. I replied, 'Oh you remembered, thank you, how are you?'

'I'm okay,' he said and asked me straight away if

I wanted to go out. I wanted to say, 'I don't think so—it's a bit dark and cold outside…' but I could sense he was nervous; and he carried on, 'I mean to go out with me this Thursday to the cinema,' he continued. 'We could watch *101 Dalmatians*.'

I replied, 'Okay what time?'

'I'll pick you up at six,' he said.

'Did anybody mention anything to you?' I asked, assuming he knew whom I was talking about.

'Ah…yes, somebody did.'

'Didn't you get anything from the Lord,' I asked?

'Well, ah… this morning when I was praying.'

'Yes?'… I said, eagerly waiting for him to say something.

'And tonight, how about you?' reversing the question in reply to my inquisition.

'I will tell you on Thursday,' I said.

'Please could you tell me something,' he begged me.

'Okay, the Lord told me your name on the 9th of October,' I replied.

'You told Joy about a name few weeks ago.' (Joy is his sister.)

'Yes I did, and I'll tell you all about it on Thursday.'

'Please can I see you in the library tomorrow?' he begged me again.

'What time?'

'What time would be best for you?'

'About eleven,' I said.

'Okay, I'll see you tomorrow.'

The following day we met as arranged. I was a bit nervous but I told him about everything I heard from God. I told him about the 'boxes' and the word I heard on the 14th of May, that 'the Lord will give me the desires of my heart,' to 'receive the gift,' and 'the Lord has not finished dealing with me,' and the verse, Psalm 75:1. Then his name, and to open the box, and 'I have not been overlooked,' 'Be patient wait and see.' I included all the dates when I told him. And all he got was the phone call from Sheryl my home group leader that confirmed it was the answer to his prayer on the morning of my birthday. He told me he had prayed many times for a wife since he became a Christian. In fact fourteen years ago, he had dated a few girls from our church. These relationships didn't last long, and he sort of lost hope and gave up looking because there was no one suitable; they were too young for him, and they just didn't get on.

Before he became a Christian he had two failed relationships, the last one was serious and he really meant to get married then, he was in his early twenties. But it didn't work out so they broke up. This time he was coming up to his 35th birthday and had received no answer to his prayers. Yet he didn't want to pick someone he just liked, even though they would be Christians too; he wanted God's guidance and approval.

I know this might sound pathetic, but a true

Christian never wants any more than God's will in their lives. You would understand if your heart's desire was inclined to do the will of God faithfully.

I was not sure of what I felt towards David at that time. I was more excited when the Lord told me his name (I was jumping about, 'He's mine, he's mine,' I said to myself) than when we were really going out together. But I had a very strong feeling I didn't want to lose him. Our relationship came so suddenly and I felt I was not really ready to change the life I had become accustomed to. Probably because my big fear was it might not work, and I actually felt I was not capable of making anybody happy or contented to stay with me forever. I was very fearful at this stage; *will it be another heartache?* It doesn't matter who ends the relationship, you will always feel hurt and rejected.

It was during that time when the lord gave me: *The cord of three strands is not quickly broken* (Ecclesiastes 4:12). The Lord was so good to me. He gave me assurance after assurance. We both believed that the word and the vision and all the dreams and everything that went with it were from the Lord.

We started to feel strange shaking sensations from our tummies whenever we were talking together, only since we started dating. We never did when we were going out bowling and never after the wedding was planned. He used to cuddle me and shook me more when I got those shaking sensations from my tummy.

Our first date started as arranged on that Thursday, the 19th of December, to watch *101 Dalmatians*. We arrived in the cinema on that afternoon—my only free time to myself while Lisa, my daughter, was at school. He paid for the ticket and I was so eager to go in quickly to the screen where *101 Dalmatians* was showing. But he stopped me for a while and told me the man had issued him the wrong tickets. 'What is it?' I said. He told me it was *Star Trek 2*. 'Did he not hear you?' I asked him, 'What are we going to do?' He was so embarrassed to kick up a fuss we watched *Star Trek 2* instead.

But in the middle of the film I felt very tired and I asked him if I could just close my eyes for a while, but I fell asleep in the middle of the film.

The second time we went to watch another film we were eager to see *Evita*, but we ended up watching *The Preacher's Wife* instead, because I wouldn't be able to pick up Lisa on time. The show was just before three o'clock and again I felt very tired and fell asleep in the middle of this film as well. I am a very light sleeper, but both times I slept in the cinema without any problems. I could hear the sound blaring out of the speakers but I was just so tired that I always missed the middle part of the films.

I find it quite amusing that I slept on the first and the second dates with the sound of the cinema speakers blaring right down my ears. I felt so relaxed in his company I never had to worry about what he would say or think, I was just being myself.

Sometimes I only had about five hours sleep a night, which I'm not used to—I always had about seven to eight hours sleep when I was on my own.

The first time I went out with David I left Lisa with a friend. I didn't tell her that David and I were going out together, and we normally went out when she was at school. So when we picked her up from school for the first time, of course she was very surprised because she had only ever seen him with me if we were with some friends, not on our own and definitely not in my home alone.

David drove us home and she was quiet at the back of the car. I think she was quite happy we didn't have to walk....I said to her, 'You know David don't you darling?' 'Yea', she said, then she sort of hung about for a while quietly; she also looked a bit nervous and set aback, then she went and hid under the table, and watched us. When she saw us talking, or sometimes when David was about to kiss me, she would stick her hand up from under the table with a tube of Pringles crisps, pop her head out and ask, 'Anyone for Pringles?' After a while it became a bit of a joke to her that every time we sat closer or if we kissed she would ask us if we wanted some Pringles and giggled.

David was a bit worried at first that he might upset Lisa. He thought she might think he was competition for Mummy's affection. Although she was only nine years old he still had to consider her feelings, and what she would think of us. But she thought he was all right, and if Mum was happy then she was happy for me. Even now she still says if I am happy she is happy for me.

Two weeks after we started going out a couple from our church invited us to go to their New Year's Eve party. We arrived laughing and joking and we were holding hands too. But the minute we entered their house we both froze for a while; every one's eyes were focussed on us. Of course they didn't know what was going on; they were as surprised to see us together as we were to seeing their stares.... I didn't know what to do and where to face; I felt like a child being caught doing something terrible and naughty....

Of course they didn't know we were going out together and to my surprise I didn't know they had invited almost the whole church. My future sister-in law had managed to tell just a few people about us so we were in for a shock. I almost pulled my hands out of his, but David gripped my hands tightly and sat with me, looking rather sheepish. Somebody in our church called him a dark horse, then someone else called me the same after a while.

We felt too embarrassed to join in the party games because everybody's eyes were on us; as though we were a television set ready to be watched. We are both shy types and almost felt like saying 'Let me hide for a while till you get used to us', but of course we couldn't. For a few months I felt a few people were trying to suss me out; I got the look that says,

'What makes you think you're equal?' Maybe just my interpretation, but that's what I felt when they were gazing at me; although some were truly happy from the bottom of their hearts for us.

Lisa's dad eventually knew I was seeing David. He hinted by saying he could feel a spring wedding in the air. 'What is your plan', he asked; 'do you plan to have a baby?' 'Steady on! We have been going out less than a month', I replied. I thought he would say some hurtful remarks against me when he found out, but he actually said, 'I hope you'll be happy, you have my blessing.' I was amazed to hear those words from him....

One day David told me when he was praying he saw a vision of himself and this was how he saw it. He was standing by a bus stop. When the bus was approaching he put his hand out but he was a bit slow and the bus did not stop, it passed by him. And he felt the Lord was telling him not to miss the opportunity. He didn't have any doubts about getting married. The only thing that made him think twice was his dad. David's father was against my marrying his son, because I was a divorcee.

That's probably why I saw him in my vision lying on the ground; he disagreed with me, not personally, but against my status and the fact that I also had a daughter. David's mum was fine with it, but since we started going out there was a tension in their home, because of his dad. Before we were even engaged officially, David's mum fished out his birth certificate in order for him to register legally at the register office, three months before the wedding. She knew how serious he was. His sister told me his mum had prayed for David a week before we talked, and she believed this was an answer to her prayers.

I was saying to David jokingly, 'The Lord didn't say you have to be my husband, but I was wondering why He told me your name? I wonder if there is another David somewhere; are you the right David I asked?' 'No other he said,' and he teased me by saying, 'Oh, it's leap year,' and gave me a wicked smile. 'I wonder if you will...'

'Propose perhaps?' I said, interrupting him. 'Ah...I have never done it before and I don't think I will do it now; but there's another leap year in four years' time. I'll see what I feel then. We don't even know if we will get on, but it doesn't matter, if we end up fighting all the time I'll just have to send you back to your mum.'

6

WAS THE WEDDING OFF?

David's father found it very difficult to accept the reality of his son joining in matrimony with a divorcee. It is stated in the Bible that anyone who marries a divorcee commits adultery. (This matter, I believe, referred to a person who divorced his wife or husband to marry another one immediately after the divorce paper came through, or divorcing a husband or wife for another person).

But my situation was different; I was divorced for over two years and was not looking for a husband, though I did ask the Lord once to find me a very good friend; someone I could rely on.

A platonic relationship would suit me best, since I promised God not to remarry. I didn't want any commitment. I just wanted a very good friend who wouldn't assume that I fancied him; somehow I felt it would embarrass me. When I promised God not to get involved with anyone, I really, really meant it.

I had quite a lot of friends who were very concerned about my being single; actually, the husband of a friend wanted to see me married to one of his friends. I would have a choice if I liked them and vice-versa but I didn't like any of them. The first reason I didn't want them was because they were not

Christians, and they were too influential for me; they were all financially secure and holding very good jobs.

Like his wife, he wanted to see me not struggling financially. He had a very good heart indeed. He took me under his wing when I needed somebody to help me; he and his wife (my friend) helped me in every way. May the Lord bless them both. The other Filipino friends of mine and their husbands were all equally good to me.

It was very important for me that anyone coming into my life would love the God I loved. Nevertheless I promised God not to marry again. And that promise I kept, until the Lord bestowed His favour on me, for He knew the real me in every way. I didn't choose David and vice versa. Although he had feelings for me he sought God's will and approval, not his own. All the words from the Lord stated that it was all right with God for me to remarry. Not my choice and not my plan, but God's.

In Jeremiah 29:11 it says: *For I know the plans I have for you, declares the Lord, plans to prosper you and not to harm you, plans to give you hope and a future.* I found out David and I prayed exactly the same prayer, 'The Lord knows me better than I know myself.' In the end he had an answer to his prayers, but I had a plan of my own.

It sounds so childish and uninteresting now, but then it was for real. I wanted to learn how to drive, because Lisa, my daughter, kept on complaining that we were always walking everywhere we went. And also I could get around and find a good job, although I didn't have any real qualifications. I believed the Lord could help me find a good job so we could go on holiday, just my daughter and I; we were happy, just the two of us.

But two weeks before Christmas 1996, I asked Lisa what she wanted for Christmas and she said, 'A dad.' She was crying as well when she was telling me this.

'But you have a dad,' I said.

'He is not always here,' she replied; 'and some of the children at my school have been bullying me because I haven't got a dad here.' That was heart breaking when I saw her crying. I hadn't realised how unhappy she was. She paused for a while then she continued, 'I...I...also want a brother or a sister, everyone has a brother or a sister but I haven't got anyone to play with.'

'But darling where would I get one, from Tesco's or Sainsbury's?'

She smiled, then she cried again so I told her, 'You have to pray, and you have to pray nicely darling; you never know, it might be delivered by Christmas.'

When David came round to our home when we used to go bowling, Lisa told me once she didn't like him. When I asked her why, she gave me a petty answer, as a child would do. 'He is always laughing at me,' she said. When she left the room I said, 'Lord she doesn't like David, I don't want anybody to come between us. Lisa will always be my priority, when you gave her to me she was my first responsibility,' I murmured. I knew children are precious gifts from God. (See Psalm 127:3 and Psalm 139:13.)

By this time I was beginning to like David a bit. One night he and a few friends picked me up from my place to go bowling. When I invited them back to my home for a drink after bowling, I noticed Lisa was making David laugh. She kept on looking at him, showing him her toys and smiling at him. David would smile and wave back at her. He could see that Lisa was a very happy child and he found her sweet and funny too.

With all the consequences we were facing due to David's father's legalistic view against divorce we found it difficult to include him in any of our wedding plans; although we invited him we both knew he wouldn't attend. His mother was caught up in the middle of it all. Our situation brought back memories of the time her eldest daughter remarried.

Eight years before I came on the scene she got married against her dad's wishes. Actually both his mum and dad did not attend her wedding. This put a rift between her and her dad. Mum was not always happy standing up for her husband; in the end she visited them and tried to alleviate the situation. Mum was there when she was needed and got on well with them and the grandchildren. Their granddad never saw them.

Once we were getting on all right and we were sure this was God's plan for our lives, David did not waste any time. Since he saw himself in a vision missing the bus, and the word the Lord told him, 'Not to miss his opportunity,' he proposed almost straight away. By the end of January 1997 we were engaged.

Once more I got another word from the Lord through a lady from our home group. She told me she was praying for me, when she saw me in a vision. I was walking in the wrong direction she thought, because I was facing the wrong way as I was walking, so she asked the Lord: 'Why is she walking the wrong way?' This was what the Lord said to her, 'She *is* walking in the right direction. The reason her face is turned the other way is because she is looking back at her past. Tell her NOT TO LOOK BACK.'

I must admit I was confused what to decide, one minute I said to myself, 'Yes I'd like to be married,' the next minute I was not sure. I felt I'd turned off my real feelings somehow. I was torn between my fears and emotions due to my past, and the reality of what I heard from the Lord.

I knew one thing for sure; if I hadn't heard God clearly, I would never ever marry again. It wouldn't matter who the other person was. Even if a real Adonis existed I would still say thanks for the offer, I am really flattered, but no thanks. I had a lot of questions on my mind like: *Would I be committing adultery if I remarried, since my ex is still alive?*

What would be the spiritual consequences; would the Holy Spirit leave me? But this is of God and not just me. The Lord told me 'HE WOULD EVEN REMOVE THE HINDRANCE IN MY PATH.' Thank you Jesus. How much more assurance would I need?

We decided we didn't need to waste any time, a spring wedding would be particularly good; and on the 12th of April 1997 we were married.

David's father did not attend our wedding as expected but his mum, his sisters and brother-in-law, together with the children were there. On the morning of our wedding I heard Dad was lying in bed, maybe praying against our wedding ceremony taking place. It was a beautiful event; even on our honeymoon we were blessed with glorious sunshine for two weeks.

There was one thing I knew, if God is for us, who can be against us? God's pure goodness found me a husband who is kind, gentle and loving and I praise God for him. It must have been the cry of my heart to have a good husband in the first place, without my realisation.

Because it says in Matt 7:7-8: *Ask and it will be given to you; seek and you will find; knock and the door will be opened to you. For everyone who asks receives; he who seeks finds; and to him who knocks the door will be opened.* The Lord was very generous; instead of giving me a friend He found me a very good husband.

When we came back home from our honeymoon we visited David's parents but his dad was not home when we arrived. David, his mum and his sister were very nervous because of my being there; I was the only one that wasn't. Because I made up my mind if his dad said anything against me I wouldn't retaliate, I'd walk out and not come back. But the minute his dad walked in the room and set eyes on me, I was accepted as part of the family, thank you Lord....

'See you again soon,' were his words when we were leaving.

'Yes we will,' I responded.

A few months after our wedding, Mum and Joy got the same word on the same day. When Mum was praying, she saw her eldest granddaughter in a vision running towards her front door and she got the word 'reconciliation'. Later, that evening Joy, my sister in-law, got the same word from her home group, through one of the ladies who prayed for her. 'Reconciliation' was the word.

Joy and I thought and discussed with each other that unless her sister became a Christian, reconciliation would be impossible. We were both wrong. *For my thoughts are not your thoughts, neither are your ways my ways, declares the Lord* (Isaiah 55:8).

Eighteen months after the word from Joy's home group, and the vision Mum had, Dad and his eldest daughter were reconciled. This happened a few days before Christmas. 'What an excellent Christmas present from the Lord to you, Mum,' I commented.

Apparently, Dad wrote a letter of apology and since then they were as close as they were before the rift. If it is God's plan and God's will, no one can hinder it. Dad was still in the same church, only his opinion had changed. You might think it was a coincidence. God promised first, it didn't matter how it happened, it happened because God said so....

When David moved in with us after the wedding, I noticed he took with him so much medicine. He said it was all natural products, about two jars; except the vitamins. He had very low resistance against common colds. Week after week he had some sort of complaint, like inflamed veins in his hands. Sometimes he was feverish and he used to get a lot of sinus headaches almost every other day.

We decided to sort out all his medicine; some of it was out of date. I suggested if he got a minor attack of hay fever not to take the medicine straight away; he should pray first (Christian practice). I had to be cruel to be kind. I didn't want David to rely on his medicine all the time.

We know medicine is from the Lord, but as a Christian I wanted to practice what I preached, for everyone's sake.

After two years of being married I saw a lot changes in David's life. First of all he got healed of his hay fever, then yeast allergies. He used to suffer badly with hay fever every summer. He used to get itchy eyes and a runny yet stuffy nose. But after an effective prayer from someone in our home group he got better.

He also used to feel his arms and legs were aching and he felt slightly feverish and very tired all the time. He didn't know he had a yeast allergy until one time, when we ran out of bread for a few days, he felt so well. But after he had eaten some bread, the symptoms were back again. That's when he realised he had yeast allergy; another prayer from our home group leader and he was completely healed.

Now he could take sandwiches to work every day without any worries or aches. God is always so good!

7

WHERE IS YOUR GOD?

At one point in our lives I was looking at our situation because my friends and other people from the church were asking if David had found a job by now. I believed the majority of people from the church had already given up praying for him to get a job. But I was more concerned about the people outside church; they were looking at us as though we were a lot worse off than them because David didn't have a job to go to. So I reasoned out with the Lord.

I don't know if one could call it reasoning. All I know was I lay my petition before God and I pleaded for His help. *Do not be anxious about anything, but in everything, by prayer and petition, with thanksgiving, present your request to God* (Philippians 4:6).

I prayed to God, 'Lord you know all my friends are looking at us and are probably thinking or saying among themselves, 'They have God, their wedding was from God so they said, but look at them. David is not well and he can't get any work.' They were probably telling themselves, 'Where is their God?'

So I prayed, 'Lord vindicate us and show us your power that you can lift us up from where we are and help us to increase. Lord, you said in Deuteronomy

8:18, *But remember the Lord your God, for it is HE who gives you the ability to produce wealth.*

And I looked back at the promise the Lord gave David through one of the home group leaders who prayed for him a long time ago. 'Lord this was your promise and this is what you said: *I will restore to you the years the locust have eaten* (Joel 2:25).

'I know you are the only one who can help us. With your great love and compassion grant us our request. I know if you can find him a wife you can find him a job too. You've got millions of ways to do it, David's ability is limited but yours is infinite. Bless us I pray and help David to find a good job with the ability you gave him, so we will increase, in Jesus' name, Amen.'

For me this was a heart-rending prayer, so on the 23rd of June 1999 I decided to fast. I always felt if anyone must come to God, he should humble himself before Him. And the only way to do that is to fast.

On the first day of my fasting the Lord gave me the words of Psalm 66:20: *Praise be to God who has not rejected my prayer or withheld His love from me.* So I said, 'Lord I am praying that David will get an interview tomorrow, through the application forms he has filled in.' He had filled in the application form over a week ago and hadn't heard anything from them. But the minute I finished praying the telephone rang—it was a job interview for the next day. This was the job he always wanted to do and it was relatively near.

I had planned to fast for three days. On the second day of my fast after I returned from my cleaning job, David was getting ready to go for the interview. He was about to eat his lunch and I was praying, ready to drink my cup of tea (I never do dry fasting I always have a drink), when I heard God say to me, 'Believe that it is yours and it will be given to you.'

I was not sure if it was my thoughts or God's voice talking to me. So I continued to pray and I heard the words for the second time. I couldn't ignore it—I knew it was from God. I was very excited and told David what I heard from the Lord. I thought to myself, *When the Lord said He has not rejected my prayer or withheld His love from me and all I had to do was to believe that David had this job, that is pretty certain to me.* I just had to believe. Thank you Lord Jesus.

When David left for the interview I prayed from the moment he left home until he came back. 'Lord,' I said, 'give David the right words to say, and let him find favour in the eyes of the person who is conducting the interview, especially when he's asked why he hasn't had a proper job for the last seven years. You know Lord, he filled up the application form with honesty and trust in you; you wouldn't want David to tell a lie. And we wouldn't want to do that either.'

When David came back he told me he had got on well with the interviewer. David is naturally very quiet; he's not always good at finding the right words when he is being fired at with questions. During the interview he told me he felt the Lord helped him to answer the questions, even the interviewer helped him to answer one of her own questions. He always thinks before he speaks; that's one of the qualities I like about him.

David told me they were really short of staff and very, very impressed with his technical ability. And they would let him know very soon. While we waited for the result, I continued my fast that I declared to God, for three days.

Four days had passed and there was no answer. Every time the postman delivered a letter we would jump up to see if it was to do with the interview but it wasn't. I then asked him to apply for another job; we wouldn't stop till he succeeded. I didn't want him to feel let down that's why I asked him to apply again to a different company, although deep down, we both felt he would get the job the Lord had promised him. After two days he was lined up for another interview with another firm; he still hadn't heard anything from the first one.

Then we decided to visit his mum. I asked her to pray that David would get a reply from the job he wanted. I told her what the Lord had said: to believe and it will be given to David. We were still believing, I explained, yet we hadn't heard from them. I didn't know what the obstacles were to our prayers, but we were desperate to hear from that office. If you haven't got anyone to ask for prayer support you can always ask your mother in-law....

On the eleventh day after the first interview, he rang an agency somewhere in Bedfordshire. The person seemed very friendly, very interested and he asked David a lot of questions. He asked if he had applied for any electronics jobs before. David told him he had been for an interview in an electronics firm in Potters Bar. The man then knew immediately what firm it was. It happened he knew someone in the personnel department.

David told him, 'The interviewer was very impressed with my technical intellect, yet I haven't heard from her and it is eleven days by now.' The man replied, 'I wonder why you didn't get the job, I will have a word with her.'

After about half an hour the telephone rang; it was the lady who interviewed David. She asked if David was still interested in the job. When he said yes, she replied, 'You could start on Monday the 5th of July. Your wife must be very pleased,' she commented in a friendly way; for David happened to mention in the interview that he had recently married.

On the same day David phoned back the person from the agency to tell him he had got the job and thanked him for putting a good word in. But the man told him he hadn't said anything to anyone yet!

After he accepted the job he also got replies from the other two positions he had applied for. It had taken four weeks for one of the firms to tell David he was unsuccessful. The other one offered him the job but he turned it down.

Sometimes we sat and thought how did he ever get that job? It's not that we doubted God's power and help. Just for him to fill in an application form and think what to write on it after seven years of being unemployed seemed a daunting task.

One thing we were sure of, for us it was impossible; but with GOD EVERYTHING IS POSSIBLE! (Luke18: 27)

I knew he was not very well physically when he became redundant from his previous job. He was working for British Telecom earning good money, but he never felt he fitted in there. Although he was good at the job and enjoyed working in all aspects of electronics he somehow felt unhappy working in that place. He had developed an inferiority complex and lost self-confidence; he felt he was being watched all the time. That's why it took a very long time for him to seek employment again. He wanted to work in a place where he could be sure the Lord had put him there. He didn't want to make another mistake of ending up in the wrong job, even though the money might be good.

It might be a very different story for a lot of people. Someone might think why would anybody seek God's help to find the right job. Because the majority of Christians like us depend entirely on God's guidance. We want our life to be in line with God's plan, not ours.

It may sound very boring for unbelievers, to walk

in the will of God. But I tell you, when I felt God's hand moving in my life what a satisfaction and contentment it was, to experience a peace that surpasses everyone's understanding and a fulfilment in life that money cannot buy. Can anyone buy happiness, contentment, peace and satisfaction? In God's care there is healing, peace of mind and freedom. There's no heavy burden in your heart and mind if you give it to Him.

For He said: *I will never leave you nor forsake you* (Joshua 1:5); *You can ask anything in my name and I will do it* (John 14:14). I always knew where God was when I needed Him. He is always a call away. He was, and always is, there for me when I need him, even for anyone else who would call to Him in spirit and in truth, if they call to Him with all their heart. In Jeremiah 29:12–14 it says: *Come and pray to me, and I will listen to you. When you seek me with all your heart I will be found by you.*

When I decided to accept Jesus into my life as my own personal saviour, protector and God of my life, I never, ever regretted it. His love is immensely comforting and reliable. Many times in my life there were wishes I wanted to ask Him, things I was just pondering in my heart, just wondering if I had to ask God or not. But the answer was there; sometimes it felt like something served on a plate. That's how good God is, if your heart is devoted to Him. 'I THANK YOU, JESUS.'

There are times when I felt God was far away

81

from me; or it was more likely to be that I was the one far away from God. It is not always easy walking the walk of faith especially if you are in the middle of any situation that you find difficult to deal with. Sometimes when I was down, I would speak His word into my circumstances. Like for instance Psalm 43:5: *Why are you downcast O my soul? Why so disturbed within me? Put your hope in God, for I will yet praise Him, my Saviour and my God.* Any word in the Bible that could relate to my situation I picked and spoke at my circumstances. It always worked for me.

When I feel God's presence somehow I wouldn't be able to exchange it for multi-millions of any currency, that's how excellent it is. Reading the Bible, listening to Christian music and praying were easy. Coming into His presence was truly fantastic; I cannot compare it to anything existing in this world. It is not a performance, it is God's goodness that brings you into His presence, for 'God is Almighty God.'

Living in a Christian way is always submitting to Him at every opportunity.

* * *

Another incident I recall was when Lisa was about four or five years old. She used to get a pain in her legs; sometimes she could not walk properly. She would limp and be in real agony. This event normally happened in the middle of the night without any apparent reason. She would wake up crying for a long time. This had happened once or twice before, but I didn't take much notice.

Then one night she had the pain again and this time it was worse than any other time. She couldn't actually walk, she tried to walk but fell on her bottom and she could not get up at all so I picked her up. I wanted to tell my husband, who was just downstairs watching the television, but what could he do? Anyway, we had had a disagreement earlier on that day; he might, I thought, just snap at me. So instead of telling him I took her back to bed and prayed. I picked up my Bible and it happened to open at the reference for healing. It was Psalm 91, so I read the whole chapter.

I read it aloud believing what I was reading would make a difference, and it did. Within a few minutes she was sound asleep and never got that pain ever again. Thank you Jesus.

Now and again if she was not well I'd pray for her, but if the pain did not go straight away (and as usual children, or anyone for that matter, don't have any patience at all), I'd tell her to pray for herself and she would do it. I knew God had answered many of her prayers. I wanted her to learn how to express herself towards God, in her own way, with sincerity and truthfulness. I know this might sound very religious for others but for me it was just I believed and trusted God that much.

Train a child in the way he should go and when he is old he will not depart from it (Proverbs 22:6).

8

OBEDIENCE

Eighteen months after we got married we decided to visit my family in the Philippines. The minute we booked the ticket I had a feeling we would face some problem; I didn't know why. And I felt the Lord was telling me to fast, so I did. Somehow I even asked my home group to pray for our journey. I told them I felt we would face difficulties; I shouldn't have told them that, nevertheless I did.

On the day of the journey the weather in England was warm for October; it was 18 degrees Celsius. So we didn't use our coats, just our thick fleeces were warm enough for us. We knew it would be colder when we got back. Joy, my sister-in-law, suggested she would take with her our coats when we got back, for she would be the one to meet us on our return.

We flew from Heathrow Airport at about five past three in the afternoon, crossing the south coast of England to Amsterdam. The journey took about forty-five minutes. We arrived safely without any hassle and we waited in Schiphol Airport to board an international flight to Manila via Kuala Lumpur. It would take us approximately fourteen hours to reach our final destination.

On the last leg of the journey, five minutes before

the plane touched down an announcement came through, 'We will stop in Kuala Lumpur for an hour and a half. Would all passengers disembark, but leave your luggage as you will not be changing planes.'

We landed safely in Kuala Lumpur. The weather was beautiful, as you would expect in a tropical country. 'Everything is fine now,' I thought to myself; I was very excited knowing in a few hours time I would be with my mum and the rest of my family. The last time I saw them was four years ago. 'Thank you Lord we are safe and thank you for this beautiful day,' I whispered to God, but at the back of my mind I thought, *Nothing is happening.* Even after we boarded the plane I always felt there would be some interference with our journey.

My thoughts shifted to the pork pie that I had packed for my brother in-law. Was it still all right; with this hot weather would it survive the journey? But this is what he asked me to bring him. It was also heavy and I just wanted to give it to him as quickly as possible.

After a while another announcement came through, 'Take your entire luggage out, all your belongings please, you are going to change planes, go to the waiting area.'

I saw a stewardess and asked her, 'What's wrong, I thought we were not going to change planes?'

'You will now,' she said, 'they will tell you why later on. Please proceed to the waiting area, thank you.'

In the waiting area at half-past twelve in the afternoon the announcement came through: 'There is a typhoon in Manila and all flights are now cancelled, your safety is our concern.'

We had to stay in the airport hotel overnight, all expenses and food were paid for and we were allowed to make one phone call for anyone who had relatives that would be meeting them in Manila. At the back of my mind I always felt there would be a form of disturbance to our journey. I felt it was not in England or Manila but somewhere else. I almost sensed this even before we left the U.K. but I didn't know it would be a typhoon; it never entered my mind that October was the rainy season.

I knew by this time my sister and brother in-law would be in Manila International Airport awaiting our arrival. I had to phone them to let them know we would not be arriving on that day. But I forgot to take their phone number with me and I couldn't remember it either. I was desperate to contact them although it would be too late anyhow. Even though there was a time zone difference it wouldn't have helped, the delays were irrecoverable. I assumed they might have heard the news by now.

I heard we would be leaving early the next morning, but the following day we did not actually leave till the early afternoon; when we did, we flew from Kuala Lumpur to Singapore; it took forty-five minutes to arrive there.

Singapore Airlines took the responsibility of flying us to Manila. On our journey we amused ourselves with the video games on the small screens in front of us, on which we could also see the route we were taking. The weather in Manila was still bad and the crew was worried we might not reach our destination because the pilot's visibility was affected. After spending forty-five minutes trying to approach the runway for landing, the pilot nearly gave up landing in Manila and announced he might have to land in Cebu instead. If this had happened, it would have meant a stay in Cebu and a domestic flight back to Manila, maybe the next day or so.

When I heard this announcement I was devastated; I then asked my daughter and my husband if they wanted to see my mum on that day. They both said yes. 'Then we have to pray and we have to pray nicely,' I told them. Watching the screen in front of me I could see the plane was just going round and round. Twenty, thirty, forty-five minutes, an hour had passed and still the pilot had failed to land the plane.

When I realised I was not getting anywhere, I made my prayer more specific. My spirit within me arose and I touched the screen with my forefinger. I pointed to this plane on the screen, right in front of me, to land in Manila and left my finger there for a long time while I was praying.

In my prayer I said, 'Lord you hold the storm, the clouds, the wind the rain and everything in this world, at your rebuke the sea becomes quiet and subjected to you; I pray Oh Lord, You will make it possible for the pilot to land this plane in Manila and not in Cebu. In the name of Jesus I pray, Amen.' After twenty minutes the plane landed safely in Manila.

When we heard the plane touch down we could hear the explosion of applause for five minutes. It was amazing! One of my friends mentioned to me once that people's applause was their expression of thanking God for a safe journey.

Praise the Lord! I felt so privileged to know God.

It was night when we landed in Manila. We were supposed to disembark at half past three in the afternoon, but due to all the upheaval, we set foot in Manila Airport at night time. It was frightening because the porter in the airport was quite abrupt; he asked us for money to call a taxi. He arranged the price with the taxi driver then we set off to Batangas, my hometown. We had only been travelling for a few minutes when the taxi driver suddenly pulled over and stopped next to a tiny booth. When I asked him why he had stopped he told us he would fill the tank with petrol, but he didn't. He disappeared for a while then came back to the taxi and set off again. We were wondering what he was up to and we thought he was scheming something and wanted to harm us.

We continued our journey, the driver recklessly speeding, although the roads were slightly flooded and it was still raining heavily. After a nerve-racking two and a half hours of driving we finally reached my hometown. Due to the bad weather and badly-lit roads I wasn't sure of the exact location of my sister's house, so I asked the driver to stop for a minute. I got out of the car to check if we were near the welding shop that I knew was next to my sister's house. I asked a boy if he knew where the welding shop was and he said we were right outside.

I went up to the front gate of my sister's house and frantically shook it, shouting my sister's and brother-in-law's names because it was locked. We arrived at nine o'clock on that night exhausted, yet safe in the care of God.

* * *

Just over a week before Christmas 2000, a day before my birthday, we were on our way to Harlow. David and Lisa wanted to get a little extra present for me. As David was driving along, the car started shuddering and jerking; the engine of the car went wrong without any specific reason and we were alarmed. David suggested I pray, so I started praying and rebuking the enemy. I commanded him, 'Do not touch the engine of the car and leave it alone. The Lord provided us with this car and you don't have any right to touch it, so back off!' I shouted, tapping at the dashboard several times while I was rebuking him. Then I started singing, 'In the name of Jesus there is the victory.' My daughter and my husband were both very quiet just watching and listening to my frantic rebukes and singing.

If anyone saw me at that moment I knew they would think I was mad, completely barmy! Lisa and David were a bit embarrassed because they thought somebody had seen me.

David pulled over and revved the car up; he wanted to open the bonnet to see what was wrong with it. But before he did, I prayed silently again, 'Lord, send us your angel to mend the engine of our car so it will run smoothly, in Jesus' name, Amen.' After five minutes of revving it up, while I continued singing 'In the name of Jesus there is the victory', he smiled and said, 'I don't need to open the bonnet, it's fine now.' I turned to both of them and declared the Lord was not only a good physician, He was also an excellent mechanic, Hallelujah! Then I changed my song to, 'God is good, all the time.' By then David had joined in singing, smiling from ear to ear as we all did. 'This car is now running more smoothly than before we left home,' he said.

* * *

A day before New Year's Eve 2000 I saw my friend's husband in the post office. We exchanged *hellos* and he told me a lot of our neighbours had had problems with their cars in the snowy weather and he asked me if ours was all right. Our car was fine thanks, I replied. I didn't tell him what had happened two weeks ago.

I glanced in the corner and saw my friend posting a parcel at the counter. I learned they would be away for a few days, so I wished them both a *Happy New Year*, kissed them and left for Watford to buy an extra present for Lisa. We were never able to go there before Christmas, as we were busy. Lisa managed to get the top she wanted and David bought me a skirt.

On our way back home I said to David, 'I saw our friends in the Post Office; they asked me if our car was all right. I said, 'Yes.'

But the minute I said yes, the car started playing up; shuddering and jerking and the engine almost stopped. 'Darling can you pray please,' David asked me.

So I prayed, rebuked the enemy and tapped on the dashboard over and over again. I warned the enemy to let go of the car engine, not to touch our car in Jesus' name! 'God forbid you to touch God's people and God's property, as we are God's property,' I professed. I threatened the enemy that God would give him a good hiding if he didn't let go of the car engine. 'Flee, in Jesus' name!' I shouted.

The car ran smoothly again after a few minutes of my frantic rebukes. My husband laughed at the threats I gave. Then I turned to Lisa and I told her, 'Darling you witnessed twice what happened to our car. If you are facing any problem at all wherever you are, call on God and pray with all your heart. God will come and help you.' I wanted to teach her the truth about trust in God.

When we got home, David told me off for thumping on the dashboard. 'You're breaking the car!' he snapped. 'I'm mending it', I snapped back at him. We both laughed.

* * *

In October 1999 I was fasting for five days. Maybe you are asking now how often do I fast? As often as I feel I should. I felt the Lord wanted me to fast at that time, but I would be facing a problem if I did because on the third day I was due to have my tooth extracted. I needed to take some sort of pain killer after I had my tooth out. (I don't take medicine or alcoholic drinks when I'm fasting.) But I felt quite strongly I had to fast—for whatever reason the Lord asked me I have no idea. The appointment had been booked several weeks previously. I felt uncomfortable with my swollen and painful gums, which had been giving me problems for months. You see if you keep on talking to God, the Lord will speak to you. Psalm 25:14: *The Lord confides in those who fear Him.* I fear to displease God and I know true Christians do. We all know, not because a person goes to church that individual is a Christian. You are a true Christian if you obey God. I can assure you, you will hear God if you call to Him with all your heart. See Jeremiah 33:3.

The dentist gave me an anaesthetic before he

pulled my tooth out. I knew I didn't have any problem about not eating; the only problem was the pain when the anaesthetic stopped taking effect.

When I went home I prayed and asked the Lord to hold the anaesthetic for twenty-four hours, so I wouldn't feel the pain. My head and face felt really hot and the side of my face where the tooth was pulled out was throbbing, but I didn't feel any pain. I was very tired and feeling rather sleepy. I don't normally sleep in the daytime when I'm fasting but this time I couldn't help it, I had to have a rest. But before I did, I uttered a prayer of protection. 'Lord,' I said, 'send me a guardian angel so the enemy cannot touch me while I am sleeping and my consciousness would not falter in acclaiming your goodness.' I am always aware that when you are sleeping that's the time the enemy can tempt or attack you.

Only after a week could I feel the anaesthetic releasing slowly. I could taste it; it was bitter and made me felt slightly sick. It was awful, but I thank God for holding the anaesthetic for a week.

* * *

When David and I were courting I developed a skin allergy. I thought everything would be fine because this relationship was from the Lord. But the reality didn't seem to fit with the situation. I started scratching and I got a lot of rashes all over my skin and I didn't know why. I prayed many times but I didn't get any better at all. Had I done something wrong against the Lord, I asked myself? We tried to stop using everything that we suspected as the problem but it didn't make any difference. We even got a prescription from the doctor and used every medicine prescribed to me. Some people from our church even prayed for me, but my skin irritation wouldn't go away.

I found out in the end I was allergic to David's deodorant. Even the soap I usually used irritated my skin during that time, but not before I met him, that's why I thought I was badly allergic to my husband; imagine that?

Then one day I was thinking I wanted to do some fasting but I didn't know what for. I heard the Lord say, 'For your skin,' so I did fast for a few days and I've been itch free ever since. Thank you Lord. It makes a lot of difference when you hear directly from God, because you have complete assurance that He is on your side. When the Lord reveals something He wants to help you and make you better.

Most of the time we do not have an answer but the Lord does. It always amazes me that miracles normally happen when you least expect them. But sometimes you have got to accept the reality of the problem you're facing before the hand of God moves. At other times you've got to expect and trust Him first before He can do anything in your circumstances. We know God is a God of love; He wouldn't leave you feeling rejected and unloved.

If you've never experienced God in your life, all of what I am writing in this book—the miracles, God's love and hearing from Him personally—will be meaningless to you. You may ask, 'But how could I experience His love, power and miracles?' If you will sincerely seek Him with all your heart, you will find Him or HE WILL FIND YOU. If you expect God's power by believing He still does miracles, you will see a miracle happen in your life, for *Jesus Christ is the same yesterday, today and forever* (Hebrews 13:8). What He did for me He'll do for you, if you dare to believe Him....

Jesus said, 'I am the way the truth and the life, no man comes to the father except through me.' It simply means if you accept Jesus as your personal saviour and protector and acknowledge that you are a sinner—yes, a sinner—then He will forgive your sins and you will experience His goodness in your life. You may say, 'But I didn't sin; what is there to forgive?' Maybe you are saying, 'I didn't commit adultery; I didn't murder,' and so on. But think about these things: Have you ever used foul language, or maybe thought badly about others, your workmates, your friends, maybe your wife, your husband, your parents or even your children? God has high standards and although you may think these are not sins, they actually are, and unless you acknowledge them before God you are still standing accused...(see Romans 3:23). *There is no one on earth who is righteous, no one who does what is right and never sins* (Ecclesiastes 7:20).

You could pray a simple prayer but you have to be honest with the Lord, for He knows what's in your heart before you even open your mouth. You can start by saying this prayer or a prayer of your own if you prefer:

Lord, I am not really sure if I know You, truly know You; but I want you in my life. I acknowledge that You died on the cross for me and that I am a sinner and want to turn my back on all my sin. Please forgive me for all the bad things I have ever done and said. Lord, would you change my life from now on; I'm accepting you as my personal Saviour and protector of my life, and the Holy Spirit to guide me and be with me forever, in Jesus' mighty name, Amen.

If you meant what you prayed, the Lord will receive you.

Maybe you knew God and you just drifted away from Him. If you want to go back, His loving arms are widely open, ready to receive you again. Just be honest with Him, ask for His forgiveness and He will restore you as His son or daughter with complete assurance of His care and His love.

Do you remember the Bible story of the lost sheep that wandered off? The owner left the ninety-nine and looked for the one that was missing. When He found it, He joyfully put it on His shoulders and went home. He was happier with the one that was returned than the ninety-nine that were safe in the fold. And how about the prodigal son's story? He walked away from his home and his father. He squandered his inheritance but when it was all gone he decided to go back home. When his father saw him from a distance he was so happy that he urged his servants to prepare a banquet for him and he restored him as a son.

It says in the Bible, Luke 15:7 &10: *I tell you that in the same way there will be more rejoicing in heaven over one sinner who repents than over ninety-nine righteous persons who do not need to repent. There is rejoicing in the presence of the angels of God over one sinner who repents.* How wonderful; the angels of God will rejoice with you.

If you believe that you have sinned against God and accept Jesus in your heart to rule, then angels of God will rejoice over you. You won't lose anything that you have now, but you will gain God's love, protection and guidance and power over anything that comes against you, if you put your trust, hope and life in His hands. He is listening and He's ready to help you, just ask.

God is a real gentle God; He will never cross over your will, only if you invite Him. He will stand and knock at the door of your heart to find out if you will let Him in, He's waiting.

Now it's your decision. Are you willing to let Him into your heart? Or will you keep Him waiting, standing and knocking? You have freewill, it's your choice.

9

THE LORD SPEAKS THROUGH DREAMS AND VISIONS

Today, Tuesday the 13th of December 2005, I feel the Lord wants me to write down one specific dream I dreamt nearly ten years ago. It was 1996, I cannot remember the month and the date. But it has come to mind quite frequently this year, specially this month of December, and I can never forget it.

This is how my dream in 1996 goes: I found myself in this ordinary place, a field; where it dawned on me in my dreams that it was the garden of Gethsemane. In my dream I was wearing my red and navy colour house dress I used to have when I was still in the Philippines, ten years before I had this dream. I didn't know how I reached this field, I just found myself there. In the next scene I saw there were a few old men. They were in a valley; about six or maybe even seven of them, dressed in an old fashioned way; it was like being back centuries ago. They were discussing something among themselves but there was no actual voice coming out of their mouths, just a few quick gestures, as if they were talking with sense and feelings, a deeper sense as if in spirit, no verbal words being spoken. I was hidden opposite them by the hillside, watching them from a distance, slightly hiding myself from them. I was all alone. Then one of the men among them stood up and I recognised him as Elijah. The minute I recognised him and whispered to myself 'Elijah,' he heard me. I was considerably too far away for him to hear me, but he pointed directly at me. The power of his point made me bow down to him with my face to the ground, speechless. With such power and authority of his action, I was forcefully brought down on my knees, as if some sort of force pinned me face down to the ground and made me kneel down speechless before him. The men in his company didn't even notice me; their backs were turned against me. Without any word coming out of his mouth, just by pointing at me it seemed a communication already, that he was rebuking me, as if he was not happy for me being a woman, mentioning his name in the company of other men.

In reality I was actually saying to myself, 'Since Jesus is the higher power in the whole universe I will not bow down to anyone except Him alone.' But even in my dreams I was saying to myself, 'I am not going to bow down to you, you are not Jesus. I am only going to bow down to Jesus,' even though I was already on my knees, with my head bowed down, surrendered and unable to utter a word to him. It really made me understand that the Lord's elect, like Elijah, truly had a power over people who didn't have the same level of calling as they had.

As I was thinking about not bowing to Elijah in my own accord and will, still in a dream, another scene came to me; I was watching the Lord Jesus and His disciples as if I were a silent observer of these men. As I was watching the Lord Jesus with His disciples, my mind spoke to the Lord Jesus, 'I will only bow down to You.' The Lord didn't completely ignore me, but walked among His disciples, showing me that even He didn't treat Himself higher than His disciples. In fact His disciples were having some sort of heated argument, but He didn't even stop them or say anything to them, He just let them continue arguing. They truly had a freedom to speak and voice out their opinions with each other. He just let them, His hands off their own cases. He was like a brother to them, there was no higher or lower among them, they were all equal to Him; no favouritism going on there. And even among Elijah's group of men, I sensed they respected each other's authority, in both groups of men, although Elijah seemed to be the leader in his group and they respected him, in both Elijah's and the Lord Jesus' parties. He never even made Himself higher than them and whatever authority they had received from God the Father and the Lord Jesus, they were free to exercise any rights they'd been given. If anyone of them required respect, they would receive it and the Lord Jesus respected their wishes, not intervening on behalf of anyone. Elijah's group of men were slightly separated from the Lord Jesus' group of men. And I was even further away from all of them.

The Lord Jesus didn't look at me or communicate

with me He just gave me a sense that He would not stop me bowing to Elijah if that's what Elijah required of me. I realised I was about twenty to twenty five feet away from them all, it was quite a considerable distance. I realised even in my dream that I was not allowed to talk to them. Women were completely forbidden to speak to any man in the presence of all male gatherings or congregation, especially in Elijah's generation.

Then I woke up with a feeling of a question in my mind. I was sort of praying and talking to God thinking, *What does it mean?* And this was what I got: if I cannot bow down to Elijah, who was older and higher than I am, then how could I show respect to the Lord Jesus when I didn't want to show respect to Elijah? It was, and still is, the hierarchy ordained by God to honour your elders among all past and present generations. That's why older people require respect from a younger generation. And Elijah the prophet of God was here on earth before I was; and if he required respect and honour from me, who am I not to give him the respect and honour due to him, for the Lord Jesus requires it from us too. And whatever Elijah decided to do to anyone in Elijah's own will and decision, the Lord Jesus wouldn't interfere or mediate or even stop him from what he required of a person or persons. In this dream I had, the Lord is letting me know it's okay to kneel to another as long as I wouldn't make him my God. He would always and *only* be the higher authority I had to honour. And in those generations past it was considered disrespectful for a woman to speak in public unless she was talking to her husband. And whatever authority the Lord gave to anyone he or she could use it according to their own freewill and privilege.

I feel the Lord Jesus was explaining to me that in Elijah's time women were not allowed to speak in the presence of a group of men, and the men required for the women to be quiet, obedient and respectful to all men, because it was considered shameful and disrespectful for a woman's voice to be heard in public.

And even the Lord Jesus treated His disciples not lower than Himself but as brothers, so what reason have I got to protest when Elijah made me bow down to him speechless. What I didn't expect was the power and authority, forcefully bringing me down on my knees, and **Elijah not saying a word just pointing at me; but with the power of his pointing he made me bow down to him....**

Now I realise it's true, if I cannot bow down to the people who have power and authority over me, how could I, a mere human, bow down to the Lord Jesus who has authority over everything.

* * *

On the 14th of January 2006, I had a dream about Lisa. In my dream Lisa was showing me her birth certificate. She was extremely happy and so amazed, she was running towards me saying, 'Look, Mum, at the meaning of my name, I've read it means "ACT BY THE WILL OF GOD"!' I said to myself in my dream that I didn't know that was the meaning of her name. Even in my dream I was amazed and happy too, just like Lisa. But in reality at that time she wasn't happy at all. And she actually had asked me, why was she born?

It reminded me of my dreams when I was pregnant with her (my only child). It was, I think, February or March 1987, it was at a pretty early stage of my pregnancy. My dream goes like this: I found myself on a dilapidated piece of concrete building with three steps outside. I was sitting on the top of the steps when I saw foreign-looking ladies, dressed up as if they came from the olden days, and Jesus was with them. They looked like Jewish ladies and the majority of them had long wavy hair, wearing old fashioned-looking clothing as if they were from the seventeenth, or even maybe eighteenth, century. The Lord Jesus was holding bunches of beautiful flowers in His hands and these ladies were almost snatching them from the Lord's hands. I was just sitting there watching them, I didn't want to join them and I also felt embarrassed to snatch any flowers from His hands. But He was as excited as these ladies were. I said to myself that I would not snatch any flowers from His hands—I felt that was rude—I would wait for Him to give me flowers, and I was thinking they do not have manners by snatching these beautiful flowers from His hand! But He didn't mind at all—in fact he was almost teasing them to be the first to get a bunch.

So I waited for Him to see if He would give me some flowers, but He didn't give me any. All of a sudden everyone disappeared. I looked down beside me and there was a bunch of flowers, maybe about five or six in a bunch; they looked really beautiful, and I was asking myself if it was for me. But obviously nobody was there to answer me and since I was on my own in that place it would be pretty obvious that it was for me. I didn't feel sure about picking it up, because it wasn't given to me. I turned my face the other way thinking what would happen if I didn't pick up this bunch of flowers, still sitting on the steps. When I looked again, all the flowers just disappeared. I was so saddened that the flowers were all gone, and I said to myself, 'I wish I had picked it up, oh how I wish I'd picked it up!' As I was thinking of what had happened, feeling really sad, a single flower dropped on my lap, a single pink flower. I think it was a carnation. It wasn't as beautiful as the bunch of five or six that was left beside me. So I was still sad, but I kept on looking at this single flower and it turned out to be beautiful on its own. I smiled in the end because it looked so beautiful on its own and I accepted that just one will do for me. Then I woke up; I don't know what this dream meant....

At that time I wasn't going to church, as I had at that time turned my back on God, though not completely because I still prayed. I couldn't truly turn my back on God completely, because I had experienced His goodness and had a few answered prayers. And I also had already heard the voice of God since becoming a Christian. When you have experienced the goodness of the Lord in your life you cannot completely ignore and just forget Him. Godly experience is unforgettable, and He's so amazing, I love Him.

* * *

THIS IS NOT A DREAM ANYMORE THIS IS REALITY: When Lisa was about four or five I was back in the church near me. I read a book entitled *Good Morning Holy Spirit*. I found out the author's mother had a dream where she was holding a yellow rose in her hand during the time she was pregnant with him, the author of this book. After reading that book I realised that flowers signify children and I knew then that the single pink flower in my dream meant I would only have one child.

I got divorced after seven years of marriage and after two years not thinking of getting married again the Lord blessed me with a husband. But before we got married I heard the Lord say to me on the 2nd of December 1996, 'Pray that you and David will not miss out on the blessing.' I feel I couldn't have the blessing without him and vice-versa. I do not know what this blessing is.

* * *

This time I had a vision which I really saw with my natural eyes: It was Sunday April 28th 2013, and we were going on holiday to Fuerteventura. The night before, I couldn't go to sleep properly, and I kept on praying because I was scared that something might happen to me or David abroad. It was only because I had heard all the news on the television about English people going abroad and getting mugged or not coming back because they were murdered etc. etc. I never mentioned to David about my fears. All I know was I kept on saying that the protection of the Lord is upon His people and since we are God's people He will protect us. We had to get up early, about two o'clock in the morning, so we could be at Stansted Airport by 4 a.m. I woke up at midnight to go to the toilet feeling restless. Then I fell asleep again and this time I had a dream: I was standing by the door of someone's house, I knew it wasn't my house. There were quite a lot of people who wanted to come in but I would not let them in. I just told each one of them, 'No, you cannot come in,' and there were these two people in my dreams that I knew but I still said to them that they were not allowed to come into this house. Then I started praying in my dreams. I said, 'I send an angel to go ahead of me in Fuerteventura, and even in the taxi he will be there with us, and that there be no spirit that will attach to us from there that is not of God, in Jesus' name.' But even when I said, 'I send the Angel ahead of me, I said to myself in the dream, 'It's God's Angel not mine, I couldn't send the Angel.' Then I woke up before the alarm went off at 2 a.m. and I did feel relaxed, not tired at all. The minute we got up I said to David we have to pray and read the Word of God, but he said to me, 'We don't have time for that now.' I said to him, 'Oh yes we do—especially with the dream I had'. And I told him my dream. So he agreed to read our daily devotions and I prayed the prayer I prayed in my dreams, but this time I said, 'Lord I'm praying that You will send Your Angel ahead of us in Fuerteventura and in the hotel we are going to stay in, to clear off everything that is not of You in there, that there be no spirit that will attach itself to us that is not of You, even in the taxi. Please Lord, send your Angel ahead of us, in Jesus' mighty name, Amen.'

Five minutes to four in the morning the taxi driver knocked on the door. David opened the door and the driver put our luggage in the boot of his taxi. But when I glanced at the taxi there was another man standing at the right side of it. I was a bit worried why this man had another passenger. I thought it might have been his mate but I could not say anything to this man as it wasn't my taxi. This man was, I feel, waiting for the driver to finish what he was doing and get in the taxi with us. I turned to David and said, 'Oh. Two of them,' but I don't think David heard me while he was locking the front door. Just before I was about to cross the road to the taxi there was this swift whitish car that passed by and the man disappeared. I reached the taxi and asked the Lord, 'Lord what is that all about?' I felt that the Lord said, 'The Angel' and reminded me of my prayer, so I was so excited at the back of the car. When we arrived at the Airport I asked David if he saw the other man. He said no. Then I asked him, 'Did you see the car that passed by so swiftly before we crossed the road? He said, 'There's not a car that could pass by; the taxi was parked in the middle of the road!' So I said to him, 'I'll tell you a secret: the Lord sent His Angel ahead of us and I saw him with my physical eyes. He just looked like an ordinary man, but he was wearing a white shirt and dark trousers, maybe denim; he looked just so normal.' He even looked similar to a man from our church, who I know is still alive today. He just looked a bit like him, just looked so normal, that's why I thought it was a mate of the taxi driver. Wow, wow, wow! I saw the Angel of the Lord, with my physical eyes! And after that, I was so excited—I wasn't scared anymore.

I asked the Lord for the meaning of my dream about these two familiar men who knew me and really wanted to come in to the house where I was. I felt the Lord was saying to me that these two familiar men represent fear and intimidation and that the house was me. I didn't tell David I was fearful to travel—I didn't let the man in (that's the meaning of the first man). The second man, representing intimidation, I also didn't let in; I didn't say to David we couldn't go to Fuerteventura because we might get mugged or not return alive—because that was what I was really feeling then. As for the prayer that 'no spirit that is not of the Lord will attach to us,' this is what happened: When we were there we saw a lot of people going to the dunes to strip off naked. We only found out that's what they were doing when we saw these naked people wandering about. Sometimes spirits do attach to people when they sort of entertain them in their minds. Men are visual and if you don't need to be affected by these spirits you should not be mixing with them, not even accidentally.

When we were in the coach on the way to the hotel, I saw all these people going to their hotels and I was thinking to myself, *I hope our hotel will be nice too*. We were almost the last ones to be dropped off. And as I was sitting in that coach I heard the Lord say, 'You won't be disappointed.' And the place where we stayed was just the right place for us, it was beautiful.

10

HOW DO YOU KNOW GOD IS THE ONE TALKING TO YOU?

Here are four examples from scripture where the Lord spoke to His people and animals in the past:

1 Kings 17:2⁻6: *Then the word of the Lord came to Elijah; 'Leave here, turn eastward and hide in the Kerith Ravine, east of the Jordan. You will drink from the brook, and I have ordered the ravens to feed you there.' So he did what the Lord had told him. He went to the Kerith Ravine, east of the Jordan, and stayed there. The ravens brought him bread and meat in the morning, and bread and meat in the evening, and he drank from the brook.*

There in the land of Samaria, Elijah was fed by the ravens with bread and meat in the morning and in the evening because of famine in the whole land. Think about it, the ravens could have eaten the meat for themselves, and given Elijah just the bread. But the ravens, no matter how many there were, obeyed the Lord for at least three and a half years—how awesome is that!

2 Kings 20:1⁻6: *In those days Hezekiah*

(Hezekiah was a king of Judah) *became ill and was
at the point of death. The prophet Isaiah son of Amoz
went to him and said, 'This is what the Lord says:
Put your house in order, because you are going to
die; you will not recover.'*

*Hezekiah turned his face to the wall and prayed to
the Lord, 'Remember, Lord, how I have
walked before you faithfully and with wholehearted
devotion and have done what is good in your eyes.'
And Hezekiah wept bitterly.*

*Before Isaiah had left the middle court, the word
of the Lord came to him: 'Go back and tell Hezekiah,
the ruler of my people, "This is what the Lord, the
God of your father David, says: I have heard your
prayer and seen your tears; I will heal you. On the
third day from now you will go up to the temple of
the Lord. I will add fifteen years to your life. And I
will deliver you and this city from the hand of the
king of Assyria. I will defend this city for my sake and
for the sake of my servant David." '*

I see in this passage that a man could change
God's plan. When God told Hezekiah that he would
die, he prayed and God changed His mind. He saw
Hezekiah weep bitterly and God heard his prayer and
healed him and added fifteen years to his life. You
see, God speaks to His people.

Jonah 1:1–16: *The word of the Lord came to
Jonah son of Amittai: 'Go to the great city of*

112

Nineveh and preach against it, because its wickedness has come up before me.'

But Jonah ran away from the Lord and headed for Tarshish. He went down to Joppa, where he found a ship bound for that port. After paying the fare, he went aboard and sailed for Tarshish to flee from the Lord.

Then the Lord sent a great wind on the sea, and such a violent storm arose that the ship threatened to break up. All the sailors were afraid and each cried out to his own god. And they threw the cargo into the sea to lighten the ship.

But Jonah had gone below deck, where he lay down and fell into a deep sleep. The captain went to him and said, 'How can you sleep? Get up and call on your god! Maybe he will take notice of us so that we will not perish.'

Then the sailors said to each other, 'Come, let us cast lots to find out who is responsible for this calamity.' They cast lots and the lot fell on Jonah. So they asked him, 'Tell us, who is responsible for making all this trouble for us? What kind of work do you do? Where do you come from? What is your country? From what people are you?'

He answered, 'I am a Hebrew and I worship the Lord, the God of heaven, who made the sea and the dry land.'

This terrified them and they asked, 'What have you done?' (They knew he was running away from the Lord, because he had already told them so.)

The sea was getting rougher and rougher. So they asked him, 'What should we do to you to make the sea calm down for us?'

'Pick me up and throw me into the sea,' he replied, 'and it will become calm. I know that it is my fault that this great storm has come upon you.'

Instead, the men did their best to row back to land. But they could not, for the sea grew even wilder than before. Then they cried out to the Lord, 'Please, Lord, do not let us die for taking this man's life. Do not hold us accountable for killing an innocent man, for you, Lord, have done as you pleased.' Then they took Jonah and threw him overboard, and the raging sea grew calm. At this the men greatly feared the Lord, and they offered a sacrifice to the Lord and made vows to him.

Now the Lord provided a huge fish to swallow Jonah, and Jonah was in the belly of the fish three days and three nights.

Then Jonah prayed and cried out to the Lord in the bitterness of soul and affliction and the Lord heard him. So **the Lord spoke to the fish**, and it vomited Jonah unto the dry land. (The Lord heard Jonah's prayer from inside the fish's belly.) So I believe wherever you are, the Lord Jesus can hear you if you cry to Him with all your heart.

This next scripture tells us that Balak, king of Moab, saw all that the Lord had done for the

Israelites and they were prosperous so he paid Balaam to curse Israel, God's people. But God was not willing for Balaam to do so. For He said, 'Do not curse whom I have blessed.' And this is how the story goes:

Numbers 22:20−35: *That night God came to Balaam and said, 'Since these men have come to summon you, go with them, but do only what I tell you.'*

Balaam got up in the morning, saddled his donkey and went with the Moabite officials. But God was very angry when he went, and the angel of the Lord stood in the road to oppose him. Balaam was riding on his donkey, and his two servants were with him. When the donkey saw the angel of the Lord standing in the road with a drawn sword in his hand, it turned off the road into a field. Balaam beat it to get it back on the road.

Then the angel of the Lord stood in a narrow path through the vineyards, with walls on both sides. When the donkey saw the angel of the Lord, it pressed close to the wall, crushing Balaam's foot against it. So he beat the donkey again.

Then the angel of the Lord moved on ahead and stood in a narrow place where there was no room to turn, either to the right or to the left. When the donkey saw the angel of the Lord, it lay down under Balaam, and he was angry and beat it with his staff. Then the Lord opened the donkey's mouth, and it

said to Balaam, 'What have I done to you to make
you beat me these three times?'

Balaam answered the donkey, 'You have made a
fool of me! If only I had a sword in my hand, I would
kill you here and now.'

The donkey said to Balaam, 'Am I not your own
donkey, which you have always ridden, to this day?
Have I been in the habit of doing this to you?'

'No,' he said.

Then the Lord opened Balaam's eyes, and he saw
the angel of the Lord standing in the road with his
sword drawn. So he bowed low and fell face down.

The angel of the Lord asked him, 'Why have you
beaten your donkey these three times? I have come
here to oppose you because your path is a reckless
one before me. The donkey saw me and turned away
from me these three times. If it had not turned away,
I would certainly have killed you by now, but I would
have spared it.'

Balaam said to the angel of the Lord, 'I have
sinned. I did not realise you were standing in the
road to oppose me. Now if you are displeased, I will
go back.'

The angel of the Lord said to Balaam, 'Go with
the men, but speak only what I tell you.' So Balaam
went with Balak's officials.

So if you are wondering why I am telling you
about these creatures that can serve humans' needs,
that talked to humans like Balaam, and obeyed God's

commands, like the ravens, the fish and the donkey—it's because all these creatures can hear God. How much more can men and women who are all created in the image of God....

* * *

The names of the characters in this part of my book have been changed, but the facts of the story are true.

This is another example of my hearing from God and it was so different from before. I heard it from the depth of my soul, a voice that spoke from my innermost being.

It was 2013 and my friend and I decided to meet up to have brunch in a café. While we were having a bite to eat, as my friend was talking I faintly heard this word, 'Who is going to have her anointing?' (Every true Christian believer has an anointing from God.) But I ignored it.

She continued talking and she told me that one time while she was praying and worshipping God, on her own at her flat, all of a sudden the whole room lit up... and there seemed to be no wall at all.... She saw a vision of herself dressed up in white; 'I'm going to get married; I was, like, caught up in heaven....'

'Did you see the groom?' I interrupted her. She said, 'No, I saw the Lord Jesus smiling at me, everything was wonderful,' she told me; 'I was very excited.'

'Was it a dream?' I asked her. She said, 'No, it was real. Everything was white; I saw the stairway, my flat didn't have walls, just white, and I'm getting married, and then I felt very tired and then I fell asleep. I woke up in the morning and I had had a goodnight's sleep.'

'What do you think the Lord is saying to you?'

'It's like I was getting married, but I only saw the Lord, it was so wonderful, I was so happy.'

And she also told me that once, when she was being prayed for at The Healing Room, the Lord Jesus gave her a tour, in a vision, of her old house. (She missed her old house, because by then she was staying in a flat.) She was elated hearing from God, for herself.

Then we roamed about in the town. She bought a few items of clothing in the shop and then it was time for us to part.

She thanked me for our time together. She said, 'Thank you for seeing me and listening to me. Thank you for today, I had a nice time.'

'Me too,' I replied, when, without any warning, I heard this voice…right deep inside me…as if it came from the depth of my soul…. 'Are you going to let her go just like that?' I replied to this voice, 'Well, yes—she only lives over there….'

'She's going anyway,' the same voice replied to me.

I was thinking to myself, *she just lives over there, two roads away from where we are standing.* As I was answering this voice my thoughts interrupted me: *I will see her again on Wednesday.* Although we never made an appointment to see each other, in my mind it seemed confirmed; I will see her on Wednesday. So we said goodbye to each other, but she turned around to me and asked, 'Do you want me to wait for you till your bus comes?'

'No, it's ok—it's too cold to hang around—I'm sure my bus is coming soon.' I turned to my right and saw my bus arriving, so we kissed each other goodbye, and as I glanced back to her as she was crossing over the road to go home, her foot just left the pavement and all I could see of her was the lower part of her leg and her foot—nothing else; no other parts of her body. From kissing her goodbye, to looking at the bus approaching, facing the same way, then glancing back to her where she was, I saw no part of her body, just her lower leg and a foot. I sort of frowned to myself, *Oh, I only saw her foot—I'm sure. Is this real?* It made me wonder for a bit, then my bus was there; I stepped inside and forgot everything I saw and heard on that day. Also this voice and vision I heard and saw, they left as quickly as they came. Even when I was inside the bus, all I could think of was the need to cook the dinner, *my husband is coming back home from work.* It never even entered my mind again, it was as if it had been automatically erased.

I wanted to text Zyra on that night but I got busy with my knitting. I was just beginning to learn how to knit. I've since got hooked on knitting, I find it so relaxing.

Three days later our friend Kara phoned me telling me that Zyra's son could not get hold of her. He had phoned her several times on Monday night to go shopping with her—they always used to go shopping together, he and his mum, twice a week—but she didn't pick up the phone. I told her I was with her last Monday, she was fine, we had our brunch together, we parted about three-ish and then we both went home. 'Oh', she said and mentioned about the gas man coming to fix her cooker on, I think she said, Wednesday. 'Hope she's fine—she's probably staying with her other friends,' Kara reassured me. The next day as I was walking home from work I smelt such a stench of a candle being snuffed out, which in my country, is a sign that someone we know has died. And as I was passing by that field I murmured to myself, 'I wonder who has died?'

The next evening I phoned Zyra, but there was no answer. I then phoned Kara, and her son picked up the phone and said he would pass the message on. I thanked him and hung up. The following day, Sunday, Kara phoned me early morning telling me that Zyra was no longer with us. Tod found out on Friday she had died. When he couldn't get hold of his mum for a few days—which was unusual for her not to even text her son—Tod went to his dad's flat and broke in because his dad didn't answer the door either. Inside his dad's flat he found his parents bodies. 'There they were,' she said. According to the news we received, his dad ended his mum's life, and then his own. I couldn't believe what I heard.

Then I remembered the voice I heard when I was with her, on that Monday, that said, 'Are you going to let her go just like that?' It kept on popping back into my head. And I was blaming myself for not staying with her—wishing so many things. I was so remorseful, but I was with her for over two and a half hours on that day and she never gave me any indication that she was going to see her ex-husband on that evening. *Oh my friend, my poor friend. I wish I had stayed with her....* I couldn't cry, I kept on thinking of the voice I heard. It wasn't sinking in, but then we went to church and knowing I would never, ever, see my friend again, my tears flowed unceasingly. I cried in the bitterness of my soul, and I still feel guilty for not staying with her.

When I went back to work on Tuesday, I heard again the word the Lord said to me, 'She's going anyway.' I realise then that the Lord allowed her to die before her appointed time. As I kept on thinking about this word, 'Are you going to let her go just like that,' the Lord gave me an impression that if I had stayed and prayed with her, I would have had her anointing. I had the chance, but it was not meant to be.

And I asked the Lord, 'O Lord, my friend, my poor friend, O Lord, did she suffer so much?' And this is what the Lord showed me in a vision: As Ken

was punching her, Zyra could see the Lord on the
Cross. She was saying to Ken, 'Look, look—the
Lord,' but he couldn't see Him. And the Lord
showed me that it was actually His body on the Cross
that received every blow that Ken was throwing at
her; the Lord Jesus body received every weight of
every pain; Ken's punches dented the Lord Jesus'
upper arm. And he was shouting at her, 'Where is
your God? Tell Him to help you and rescue you from
me,' taunting her as he threw every blow at her body.
But the Lord didn't show me what he used to kill her.

Then another scene came: Her body was leaning,
propped up on the side of the bed, and the Lord Jesus
was arranging her body—showing Ken He was re-
arranging, moving her body. And he was sort of
questioning and blaming the Lord Jesus, 'Why didn't
You show Yourself to me. Why didn't You show
Yourself to me earlier, when I was...I would
probably have stopped.' He was probably remorseful
for what he did....

But now Ken knew without a shadow of a doubt
that there is God; he saw the Lord Jesus with his
physical eyes; and he could never deny anymore that
there is no God. He never had any excuse that what
he saw of the Lord Jesus wasn't real. He could not
excuse himself for what he did; he knew then it was a
great sin he had committed against his wife and
against God. In the end he knew he had sinned and
he didn't have any more excuses for himself to
vindicate his actions.

He knew he could never face anyone again, including their own children, because he knew if he could get away with lying to people, he could never get away from the truth—the scene he just witnessed of the Lord Jesus arranging his wife's body. That's when he decided to end his life.

He was not that bad all the time; he helped to bring Zyra's three children to the U.K. for which she was always very grateful to the end. But good work cannot save the soul of a man from the judgement of God....

If he was remorseful and asked for the Lord's Jesus forgiveness, I'm sure the Lord Jesus will forgive him, even though the Lord saw what he did to Zyra. The Lord looks at the heart, so from the minutes or hours with his mind and his heart not knowing, to seeing the Lord Jesus, must have made an impact in his life.

* * *

The Lord confides in those who fear him; he makes his covenant known to them (Psalm 25:14). Confide: means to disclose secret or personal matters in confidence. How could we ever flow in our Godly business if we never hear God talk to us? As a Christian you should expect and experience these matters, for this is your confidence that God is with you. It is every true Christian's assurance that God is equipping them and communicating to them. Our

<u>Almighty God is not dumb or numb</u>. He has senses just like us and more; we only have what we know. He is an omniscient, omnipotent and omnipresent God; that's why he says in his word, 'I will never leave you nor forsake you' (Joshua 1:5). The Lord himself spoke to Joshua (see v.1–9). And in Hebrews 13:8 he says He is the same yesterday today and forever, do you get the idea? If God spoke to Noah, Abraham and Moses in the Old Testament He could speak to you and me now, in this present time, through the Holy Spirit. Jesus Christ, His son, spoke to his disciples during His time here on earth, and He can still speak to you and me in the present and future time; He is an everlasting God.

As for all who question if God really speaks, see Exodus 20:18 & 19, Job 11:5, Isaiah 28:11 and Luke 1:18–20. You would know when God speaks because it would correlate with his words in the Bible, or you would get something from people in the church who didn't even know who you are; or maybe a song or the word of prophecy from the congregation. If you are not a Christian and even if you are, and not sure of what you heard, and you cannot see it in the Word or you didn't hear anything at all, be wise and step aside, wait and check whether it is good. If it doesn't harm anyone it would more likely to be from the Lord. But all in all, if you're really seeking God with all your heart to reveal it to you He would do so, because He is a God of order, not a God of confusion. Another thing, you would feel it in your spirit if you were a true Christian. Still, if you are aware of what it says in 1 John 4:1–3: *Do not believe every spirit, but test the spirits to see whether they are from God, because many false prophets have gone out into the world. This is how you can recognise the spirit of God: every spirit that acknowledges that Jesus Christ comes in the flesh is from God. But every spirit that does not acknowledge Jesus is not from God. This is the antichrist.* And the result of what you heard would determine the outcome. If it is good, it is from the Lord, and if it's bad, then it's not.

Most of the time when you make up your mind, if you are determined and certain of what you are to do, God will speak to you if He doesn't want you to go ahead with it. He will speak to you clearly; sometimes it will be very different from what you are actually thinking and feeling. You will have peace when you hear God's voice and if you are in doubt and you continue talking to him He will let you know. Remember, the Lord confides in those who fear him, the ones who eagerly seek his will.

The Lord is the very best friend you can ever have. He will confide in you, change your heart's desire if it's not right for you, protect you and be with you always. You will also get a gut feeling, as we Christians call it, some sort of sensation in your tummy, when what you're thinking or feeling, or what you heard, is from the Lord.

EPILOGUE

And today, Monday the 21st of November 2016, I remember, or the Lord has reminded me, that those events I wrote about in the first four chapters of this book were actually given to me by the Lord in a vision. Because I could never remember everything in my life when I was little. (It's different now I journal my days' events, especially when I hear God.) But I know some people who will read this book might think it was all my raw thinking and I gathered a few thoughts to make it sound an eclectic sort of writing. But the truth is, it is almost as if it were dictated to me by the Lord in a vision when I was writing those four chapters during 1999—that's when I started writing the first part of this book. When I was writing the events I could see a vision and I only realise now, today, that it was a vision. All I remember then, back in 1999, was the feeling came back to me as I wrote my experiences in life, like the little footpath I was supposed to pass by and the voice that hindered me from doing so. Also the lines of candles where my one was the shortest one of all, the ladies in the garden tending it who didn't speak but led me to a place where I saw my brother's graveyard. My dog that went missing and was given a second life. The ring that was lost in the sea and found after I prayed. Today, the 21st of November 2016, this was revealed to me as I was lying in bed, before reading my daily devotions.

I was born in Cuta, Batangas City, in the Philippines; the youngest in a family of seven children. I became a born-again Christian in my teens. My mum was my inspiration, she was and always will be. I consider her to be the person who made me believe that God is real.

I got married in 1986 and came to England and had my daughter. I joined a local church in July 1991 and I am still a member of the same church to this day.